ENGLISH LANDSCAPES
W G HOSKINS

British Broadcasting Corporation

Acknowledgement is due to the following for their permission to reproduce illustrations in this book. References are to plate numbers.
Aerofilms, 5, 38, 65, 80, 83; J. Allan Cash, 16, 45; Douglas Allen, 22; Hallam Ashley, 24, 34; Colin Bord, 69; British Railways, 73; British Tourist Authority, 8, 46; P. A. L. Brunny, 40; Cathedral Library, Exeter, 10; Brian Chugg, 29; Eric de Maré, 79; Frank Emery, 70; Exeter City Council, 68; Tony Hutchinson, 81; Peter Jones, ii, iii, iv, vi, vii, viii, back cover; A. F. Kersting, 43, 54, 63, 84; Lancashire Life, 44; Angus McBean, 15, 26, 41, 42; National Monuments Record air photograph (Crown copyright reserved), front cover; David Paterson, I, V; Museum of British Transport, 71; Public Record office, London, 9; A. Raistrick, 30, 60; Royal Commission on Historical Monuments, 13, 52, 66; Norman Scarfe, 59; Kenneth Scowen, 49; Edwin Smith, title page, 1, 2, 6, 17, 19, 21, 23, 25, 39, 47, 48, 50, 61, 76, 78; J. K. St Joseph, Cambridge University Collection, 3, 35, 53, 75, 82; University of Leicester, 58; University of Newcastle (photo Dr N. McCord), 33; Western Morning News, Plymouth, 74.

The maps were drawn by Nigel Holmes

Published by the British Broadcasting Corporation, 35 Marylebone High Street, London W1M 4AA
ISBN 0 563 12407 5 First published 1973. © W. G. Hoskins 1973. Printed in England by Butler and Tanner Ltd, Frome and London

The picture on the front cover shows the village of Reach in the Cambridgeshire fenland. Reach was the medieval river-port for Cambridge (chapter 8). Reach Lode (at the bottom left) is even older, a Roman cut leading to the navigable river Cam. The massive linear defensive earthwork of the Devil's Dyke runs for more than seven miles. It is probably late Roman or post-Roman in date (see also plate 66).

Back cover: Fountains Abbey, founded in 1132, was endowed with thousands of acres of moorland in the Malham area of the West Riding. These were developed as vast sheep-ranches in the twelfth and thirteenth centuries (chapter 2) and remain almost unchanged to this day. The name of Fountains Fell (background) commemorates this ancient association.

Title page: Clopton Bridge, Stratford-upon-Avon, was built by Sir Hugh Clopton about 1480–90. He was a rich mercer in London and mayor in 1492. Like many successful men who came up from the provinces he remembered his native town and built this superb bridge over the Avon. Many others from the provinces founded grammar schools in the places where they had been born.

CONTENTS

SELECT BIBLIOGRAPHY

Allison, K. J. (and others), *The Deserted Villages of Northamptonshire* (Leics. Univ. Press, 1966)

Allison, K. J. (and others), *The Deserted Villages of Oxfordshire* (Leics. Univ. Press, 1965)

Beresford, M. W., *History on the Ground* (Lutterworth Press, 1957)

Beresford, M. W. and St Joseph, J. K., *Medieval England: an aerial survey* (C.U.P., 1958)

Beresford, M. W. and Hurst, J. G., *Deserted Medieval Villages* (Lutterworth Press, 1971)

Bonser, K. J., *The Drovers* (Macmillan, 1970)

Booker, Frank, *Industrial Archaeology of the Tamar Valley* (David & Charles, 1967)

Bowen, H. C., *Ancient Fields* (British Assn, 1961)

Cracknell, B. E., *Canvey Island: the history of a marshland community* (Leics. Univ. Press, 1959)

Crawford, O. G. S., *Archaeology in the Field* (Phoenix House, 1953)

Emery, Frank, *The Oxfordshire Landscape* (Hodder & Stoughton, 1973)

Finberg, H. P. R. (ed.), *Agrarian History of England and Wales*, vol. 1, pt. 11 (C.U.P. 1972)

Fowler, Elizabeth (ed.), *Field Survey in British Archaeology* (Council for British Archaeology, 1972)

Fowler, P. J. (ed.), *Archaeology and the Landscape* (J. Baker, 1972)

Hallam, H. E., *Settlement and Society (South Lincolnshire)* (C.U.P., 1965)

H.M.S.O., *Field Archaeology* (O.S. Professional Papers, New Series, no. 13, 1963)

Hooper, Max (and others), *Hedges and Local History* (National Council for Social Service, 1971)

Hoskins, W. G., *The Making of the English Landscape* (Hodder & Stoughton, 1955)

Hoskins, W. G., *Leicestershire: the history of the landscape* (Hodder & Stoughton, 1957)

Hoskins, W. G., *Provincial England* (Macmillan, 1963)

Hoskins, W. G., *Fieldwork in Local History* (Faber, 1967)

Hoskins, W. G., *Local History in England* (Longmans, new edn 1972)

Hoskins, W. G. and Stamp, Sir Dudley, *Common Lands of England and Wales* (Collins, 1963)

Hunter, John, *The Essex Countryside: a landscape in decline?* (County Hall, Chelmsford, 1972)

Lambert, J. M. (and others), *The Making of the Broads* (R.G.S. Research Series, no. 3, 1960)

Millward, R. and Robinson, A., *The Lake District* (Eyre & Spottiswoode, 1970)

Moore, John, *Laughton: study in evolution of the Wealden Landscape* (Leics. Univ. Pres, 1965)

Newton, Robert, *The Northumberland Landscape* (Hodder & Stoughton, 1972)

Phillips, C. W. (ed.), *The Fenland in Roman Times* (R.G.S. Research Series, no. 5, 1970)

Raistrick, Arthur, *West Riding of Yorkshire: the making of the landscape* (Hodder & Stoughton, 1970)

Rowley, Trevor, *The Shropshire Landscape* (Hodder & Stoughton, 1972)

Scarfe, *The Suffolk Landscape* (Hodder & Stoughton, 1972)

Spufford, Margaret, *A Cambridgeshire Community: Chippenham* (Leics. Univ. Press, 1965)

Steane, John, *The Northamptonshire Landscape* (Hodder & Stoughton, 1973)

Thorpe, H., *The Lord and the Landscape* (O.U.P., 1965)

Taylor, C. C., *Dorset: the making of the landscape* (Hodder & Stoughton, 1970)

Taylor, C. C., *The Cambridgeshire Landscape* (Hodder & Stoughton, 1973)

Thomas, Charles (ed.), *Rural Settlement in Roman Britain* (C.B.A. Research Report, no. 7, 1966)

Todd, A. C. and Laws, Peter, *Industrial Archaeology of Cornwall* (David & Charles, 1972)

INTRODUCTION

Fifty years ago I used to spend my holidays in a then remote, and still beautiful, bit of Devon. There was no village, only the squire's house (and the Fursdons had been living there since the time of Henry III and were still there), the church and the smithy and the school, and beyond that a landscape of scattered farmsteads, shining in the sun in their green combes for they were mostly built of cob and then whitewashed. The lanes wandered between high hedgebanks, turning abrupt corners and just wide enough for one cart; the fields varied in size and shape but usually made very irregular patterns.

Even then I felt that everything I was looking at was saying something to me if only I could recognise the language. It was a landscape written in a kind of code. For years I made notes from such great unintelligible authorities as Domesday Book or from classic works like Maitland's *Domesday Book and Beyond*, and could hardly make head or tail of it all. Domesday Book, which I knew was describing the landscape I was looking at as it was twenty years after the Norman Conquest, was written in an old script and in Latin, and more than that in a terse sort of shorthand. I did not know I was really jumping in at the deep end, into waters that more learned scholars than I still fail to plumb fully.

Moving to West Yorkshire and to the Midlands, in my first jobs, I encountered totally different sorts of country, which made me see even more clearly how different my native landscape was from others. The unpeopled green pastures of Leicestershire, the wide straight grass-verged roads, the very regular field-pattern, some skinny hedges (to me), asked quite different questions.

The years went by but still there came no book which deciphered the many landscapes I explored. Answers came there none. In the end I decided I should have to write my own book and try to produce my own answers. The result was *The Making of the English Landscape* in 1955. It covered most of the ground and still stands as the pioneer book on a new subject, the history of the landscape. But I became aware as I continued my explorations on foot around England that I had not thought of all the possible questions, let alone given all the answers. Seventeen years later someone in the BBC came across the book (authors are accustomed to this sort of time-lag) and decided it would make a good television film. I welcomed the opportunity to try a new kind of message, though it was perhaps too big a subject – too many themes – for a single programme.

After that came the request to write a special book on *English Landscapes* to go with the film. Note the plural, for I had long ago perceived that there was not just one landscape to explain but as wide a variety as could be found anywhere in the world, certainly within that small compass. One might easily find a hundred landscapes, each with its own distinctive character and history. It is a matter of geology, topography, climate, and the historical facts of land-ownership, even to obscure customs of inheritance. The geological map of England is highly complex, changing its colour every few miles especially if one is travelling across the grain of the land. It is, too, generally a tumbled country with few large stretches of sameness (and even they, like the Fens, vary to the trained eye). Climate plays an obvious part over he centuries, chiefly in the form of water – ponds, springs, streams. Within these physical limits, men and women have fashioned the local scene according to their human needs. Sometimes one can pass through five or six centuries in traversing half a dozen parishes.

I welcomed the opportunity to write the book, because it gave me the opportunity to revise some of my original ideas, to put in some of the many things that had to be thrown out of the film for lack of time, and to air a few new ideas for the first time. Some of these ideas, such as the powerful imprint made upon the landscape, more in some parts of England than others, by prehistoric man and by the Romano–British, came from discussion with what I may venture to call my pupils, whose ideas (as in a good university) were beginning to outstrip my own at times elementary explanations. I had dismissed the prehistoric and Roman contribution to the early landscape far too briefly in my own book back in the 1950s, merely because it was not obvious at first sight. This I learnt above all from Christopher Taylor's brilliant book on the Dorset landscape; and I learnt something fresh from half a dozen others in their different ways.

From these encounters, whether in my own quiet study in a leafy Exeter road or on the salt-marshes of Norfolk or the steel-grey seashore of Suffolk, or wherever I was in the most beautiful country in the world – not forgetting France – I was always learning something special. But above all, there were two leading ideas – not specially new perhaps but becoming more and more deeply impressed upon my mind. These were that in most parts of England *everything is older than we think*. And going with that, the idea of the impressive continuity of English landscapes. There are places where one treads on three thousand years of history, sometimes four thousand or more. How could one bear to live in a country with only a hundred or two hundred years underfoot, above all bear to die in it?

The landscapes I looked at many years ago were even then more than just scenery. I wanted to know what they were saying. Now I know something of the code and how to decipher it. In his third lecture on Landscape, Constable – that beloved and most English of painters – quotes:

> It is the Soul that sees; the outward eyes
> Present the object, but the Mind descries.

Then he adds a sentence that could be the theme of this whole book in so far as I have been successful in conveying it:

> *We see nothing till we truly understand it.*

THE LANDSCAPE OF SETTLEMENT

For such a small country England shows a remarkable variety of distinctive landscapes. This applies no less to the patterns of human settlement. Even ruling out the industrial patterns, which are of relatively late growth, the one-inch Ordnance maps show in some parts of the country a pattern of villages which most of us assume is the 'typical' form of human settlement for the country as a whole. We think loosely of the countryside as 'village England': but it is vastly more complicated than this. There are wide areas where the village is a rarity on the ground, where the parish church stands alone, with perhaps an inn or a school beside it, to mark some sort of centre; but the parish itself shows a scattering of farmsteads standing alone on their hillsides or in their combes, and here and there farmhouses in pairs, or in a small group of three or four clustered together to form a hamlet.

Not so long ago we thought that the village pattern was typical of the Lowland Zone, the eastern half of England, while the farmstead and hamlet country lay in the so-called Highland Zone to the west. The frontier was roughly an imaginary line drawn across the map from the Tees in the north-east to the Exe in the south-west. But the picture even on the map, without delving any deeper, was full of contradictions. Thus in eastern England, to take but one example, numerous Suffolk parishes show a landscape more typical of the West – a lonely church, and a score of scattered farmsteads; and Norfolk too has scores of lonely churches, out in the fields, many in ruins. On the other hand, even in the 'Celtic West' one can find substantial nucleated villages, though not so frequently as in the Midlands. However, before peering into the microscopic detail of a region, we can still make the generalisation that the village *is* more characteristic of the drier arable lowland east of England, and the hamlet and single farmstead more common on the wetter, hillier, and pastoral western side. But there is nucleation and dispersion to some degree in all parts of England.

At one time this was explained by what one called racial history. The hamlet and single farm were supposed to be characteristic of 'Celtic' peoples who preferred to live in that way; the village was thought to be the typical form established by the Old English moving into the eastern side of England from the fourth and fifth centuries onwards. Behind this lay a more sophisticated explanation related to the major differences of farming. In predominantly arable country, families tended to live together in villages because of a basic shortage of capital equipment, above all the eight-ox plough-team. Few families possessed their own unit. Several households contributed the oxen to make up a single team. Again, arable farming under the open-field system which prevailed in Europe for many centuries required co-operation at every season of the farming year, a co-operation secured in most places by scores of by-laws which all had to obey. And more than that, the clearance of new land from the surrounding woods, heaths, and marshes also required co-operation, not only of one village, but often of several villages working together as in the construction of the dikes of the marshlands and the Fens. The upkeep of these vital dikes also demanded the same co-operation over the succeeding centuries.

On the other hand, as one moves westwards the village becomes rarer because the farming is mainly pastoral. No capital equipment was needed, not even special buildings at first, for animals and men lived under the same roof in the 'long house', an ancient type which can still be seen on and around the south-western moorlands. No need to co-operate, no community rules. The pastoral farmer was his own boss and could live where he liked, provided he had water and shelter. So we get the isolated farmstead, probably from Iron Age times onwards. The hamlet, where three or four, and sometimes more, farmsteads were grouped together, is harder to explain. It could have started by the division of a given piece of land between two or three sons living near the ancestral homestead or it may have been settled as a small group right at the start. Yet it never grew beyond a certain point, never became a village with its own church and later on its own small shops. It remained a distinctive type of human settlement, particularly in Wales.

The village was settled at one go by a small group of families who often took their name from a leader – thus Peatling in Leicestershire takes its name from 'Pēotla's people'. They looked first of all for an unfailing water-supply. The most obvious supply would be a stream, and the Celts, with good reason, worshipped many streams as gods; but there were also unfailing springs where a permeable soil and an impermeable one met. Then there were ponds, especially valuable in high and otherwise waterless country. Ashmore in north Dorset (plate 5) is a splendid example of this kind. There are others on these chalk downlands such as Buttermere in Wiltshire, well over 800 feet above sea-level, or Dummer in Hampshire, or Imber in the deep heart of the Wiltshire chalk, where the earliest settlers pitched their tents, so to speak, around the pond, and stayed for a thousand years. Many of these villages were well established before the first Christian church appeared on the scene, so that it now lies on the edge of the village as at Ashmore, Dummer, and Buttermere. In apparently dry country like the chalk downlands there was yet another source of water, and that was deep wells. On many Iron Age and Romano-British upland sites this was certainly true. General Pitt-Rivers excavated two such wells at the Romano-British village of Woodcutts in Dorset, one 180 feet deep, the other 120 feet.

Next to a good water-supply a dry soil for building was generally essential, though some west Cambridgeshire villages planted upon heavy ill-drained clays put a moat around every house to drain the site, as at East Hatley, where most of the moats, or the remains of them, can be traced to this day. But for the majority of villages a dry, usually gravelly soil was the next thing they looked for after a good water supply. Often the two essentials went together, as on the glacial sands and gravels of east Leicestershire which rested on the impermeable boulder clays (plate 4). Here the overlying sands and gravels gave a dry site for building, and at the junction of sands and clays springs burst forth from the earth. In medieval times each of these useful little springs had its own name, now mostly forgotten, with its own clientèle. Some of these springs had a massive flow of water, as can be seen to this day at Stogursey in West Somerset. Most villages also looked for a sheltered site and many lie in gentle hollows that cut off the worst of the English weather. But recent excavations have modified our ideas about even this apparently elementary observation. Some upland sites, apparently open to every wind that blows, show evidence of long prehistoric and later occupation.

The village is, we now know, a very complex form of settlement. We always knew that to study it in its present form, on the map, even before the 'housing explosion' of recent years, could be a misleading kind of evidence. Even the first editions of the Ordnance map (usually dating from the early nineteenth century) were not good enough for this purpose. The oldest maps we have of village-shapes date from the late sixteenth century when the art of surveying (for big landowners) had developed to give us a graphic picture of the landscape four hundred years ago. Yet even if the village had roughly the same shape then as now, it is still not good enough evidence. Recent work on deserted village sites, where the ground is already cleared for exploration, have produced some shattering results for our ideas about village morphology.

Mr J. G. Hurst, in *Deserted Medieval Villages*, has demonstrated that we cannot jump to conclusions about the original shape and size of a village from even the earliest maps. Archaeology has shown that the late Saxon and early medieval village was in a continual state of flux, not only in the replanning of house-sites and even of the manor house. Indeed, the original church could be moved to a new site for the sake of some large-scale rearrangement. New streets could be formed, a whole village-shape altered, at dates when only archaeology and not maps can produce the evidence. The extreme complexity of landscape-history and the various phases in the settlement within a single parish has been shown in a model paper on Whiteparish in Wiltshire, by Christopher Taylor (*Wilts. Archaeological and Natural History Magazine*, vol. 62, 1967). Taylor shows that though the name Whiteparish is recorded for the first time only in 1289, the site of the present village, and other settlements within the parish, were already occupied during the Roman period. So were certain village-sites in the Dean valley immediately to the north.

The complexity of the landscape of settlement is also being brought out in a large-scale series of excavations at Chalton in Hampshire by the Department of Archaeology at the University of Southampton. Within this single parish more than 150 sites have been found, ranging from the neolithic to the present day. Three of these sites are of the early Saxon period, and all lie on ridge-tops in a most unexpected location.

It is becoming abundantly clear that though many villages bear today an Old English name, they stand upon sites that were first chosen in Roman times, if not earlier. Everley, in Wiltshire, is a hill-top village on a Romano-British site. It is first recorded in a document of 704, but just to add to the confusion it is not named in Domesday Book in 1086. Almost certainly this was because it was silently included under some other manor at that date.

This is one of the many pitfalls of the subject, and only microscopic studies of single parishes or small districts will eventually enable us to write the true history of a settlement and of the landscape around it. Upper Upham, near Aldbourne in Wiltshire, is a fine Romano-British site, amid contemporary fields, with the deserted village of Upham on top of it. A single farmstead of seventeenth-century date carries on the farming of some two thousand years.

We must be careful, however, in talking about complete continuity of farming since Roman times or earlier. A quite remarkable example of an Anglian village tucked neatly inside a Roman fort (plate 7) occurs at Piercebridge on the banks of the Tees. Whether or not there was any break in the habitation of this site we do not know. Certainly the Roman name of *Magis* changed to the Old English name of *Piercebridge* but even this evidence is far from decisive. The Roman site may never have been completely abandoned even though it changed its name. After all, we know of many instances where well-established Old English villages changed their name merely because a new overlord took over. So, for example, Northworthy (a pure English name) became Derby after the Danish conquest of the Midlands. Many Midland villages with Scandinavian names today have produced archaeological evidence of an earlier settlement in the form of Anglo-Saxon cemeteries: but the Anglo-Saxon name has disappeared without a trace.

The village is the completed expression of centuries of colonisation and change, the end product of man's adaptation to natural conditions in a given place. There is clear evidence in many places that the process began in the Iron Age, even before the Romans came. I now suspect indeed that some of our villages stand upon sites first chosen by Bronze Age farmers – perhaps even neolithic – but the evidence is deeply buried under living villages, layers down, and will not easily come to light.

1   West Penwith (the Land's End peninsula) is rich in prehistoric remains, not least in Iron Age villages such as Chysauster. Being built of granite, they have tended to survive, though heavily overgrown by tough moorland vegetation. These sites were occupied by tinners and farmers, a dual economy that persisted in mineral-bearing regions down to modern times. They were occupied from the first to the late fourth century AD and then abandoned. Chysauster, excavated by the Ministry of Works in 1931, is the best of the known sites and is open to the public. Other fine sites are known but not yet excavated.

2   In various parts of England there survive remarkable patterns of cultivation terraces, often called lynchets. They were first recognised on the chalkland slopes of Sussex and Wiltshire. In the north of England, upper Wharfedale round Grassington, and the moors near Malham (shown here) are another classic area. They are difficult to date precisely and indeed were probably in use for many centuries. Once called 'Celtic fields' on the Ordnance map, they are now safely described as 'ancient field system'. Those shown here are pretty certainly prehistoric in origin.

3   An abandoned Romano-British village site at Bullock's Haste in the parish of Cottenham (Cambridgeshire). There are dozens of Romano-British sites in this area, but this is the only one to survive as visible earthworks. The Roman canal known as the Car Dyke runs diagonally across the middle of the site.

4   East Leicestershire is largely covered by Boulder Clay deposited by glaciers in the last Ice Age. It gives a heavy, damp soil, quite unsuitable for building. Fortunately, the glacier also deposited islands of sands and gravels on top of the clay, and on these dry, easily-worked islands the Old English founded their villages and created their first fields.

Glacial Sands and Gravels
Boundary of Boulder Clay
Streams

Houghton
-on-the-Hill

R. Sence

Galby

Roman Road

Kings Norton

Great
Stretton

Little Stretton

5   Ashmore in north Dorset is perhaps the perfect example of a village centred upon a circular pond. It stands more than 700 feet above sea-level. The pond may well have been used in prehistoric times: even now all roads lead to it. The first settlement may go back to Celtic times, though the village is not recorded by name until Domesday Book (1086). Then it appears as *Aisemara*, meaning 'ash-mere', the pond where ash-trees grew. The parish church can be seen well away from the pond, a little above and to the right.

6   The village pond at Newton in the East Riding. Newton – 'the new village' – was probably a daughter-village settled from an older place. There are several Newtons in the Riding, two of which are 'lost villages'. And several Newtons are recorded in Domesday Book, so the word 'new' in the English landscape is a very relative term indeed. If the eleventh century is 'new', how old is 'old'?   15

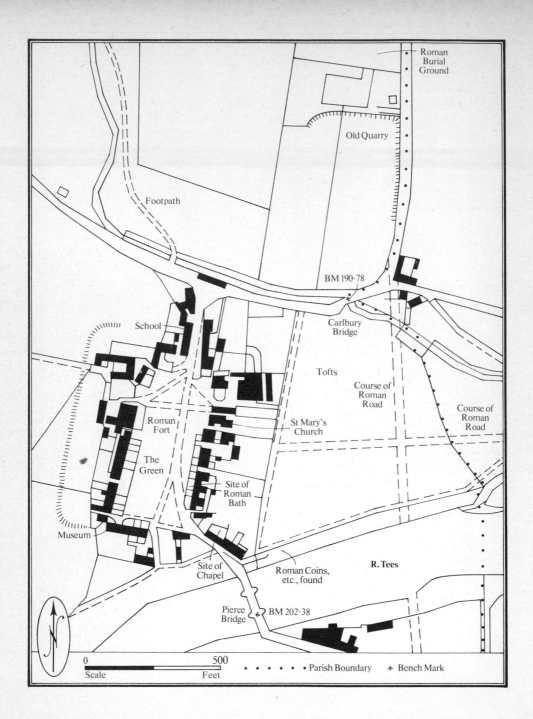

Roman
Burial
Ground

Old Quarry

Footpath

BM 190·78

Carlbury
Bridge

School

Tofts

Course of
Roman
Road

Course of
Roman
Road

Roman
Fort

St Mary's
Church

The
Green

Site of
Roman
Bath

Museum

R. Tees

Site of
Chapel

Roman Coins,
etc., found

Pierce
Bridge

BM 202·38

0   500
Scale   Feet
· · · · · · Parish Boundary   ⚓ Bench Mark

7   Piercebridge, on the northern bank of the Tees, occupies a dry terrace at a convenient crossing of the river. Though it bears an Old English name, the village is neatly tucked inside the ramparts of a Roman fort *(Magis)* and the Roman gateways are still used as entrances to the village. Whether there was any break in the continuity of the site cannot yet be proved, but only two miles north-east of Piercebridge lies Walworth, 'the homestead of the Britons', showing that here at least the native British survived the Anglo-Saxon Conquest. A bridge is recorded here as early as c. 1050.

8   Arncliffe, near the head of Litton Dale in the West Riding, takes its name from 'eagles' cliff'. The name takes us back to an earlier world when eagles nested on these precipitous walls of Mountain Limestone. Arncliffe is built round the perimeter of a large green, with entrances to it from all points of the compass so that cattle and sheep could be driven in from the fields in case of attack. Note the pump on the right: the fountain and origin of the Anglian settlement.

17

+ In xpi nomine atq; uirtute fugia in tuendo pspectu caput lapsusq; con dicionis humane dequa aecclfiastes: Uanitas uanitatu
in quid et omia uanitas. et ido mepicanda se eterna caducis; dicente ueritate. Thesaurizate uobis thes aurios in celo. et etra.

Qua ppt ego adelstanus rex monarchus totius bryttannime in rule plante do. aliqua pufuy particula id est etiam mansium ubi
ignostici uocitant topper ham. libent con cedo ad monasteriu sci petri apli exoniensis aeccle p remedio anime mey in eternam
liberitate habendi quam dru xpiana pmaneat. In munif amodo iste ager p maneat ab omi censu regali excepta communi labore
quod notu ÷ omnib; Siqr amodo hanc npam donatione ammoueat. sciat se do contra raciu ipse non mihi. quia abillo potestatem
accepi. Territoria aute ist arum agru hec st. Ærest fram topper oyian up on exan on hone ntapan team pol. hanon up on exan horine of
exa on ha smala lace. of hære lace est on exa. hanon up andlang exa on hone uppian team pol. hanon upon exan streau od pole. upp of
pole on hone taldan herpad to dypan threope. hanon sud on pynpold up on sreu on pyndeles cumb midde peapone up on ha pypian.
hanon andlang die on hone peig east andlang peiges on hære die hypnan andlang die ut on clyse. andlang sreeames est on topper oyian
his synd hære ante gypdeland ge maeid et aesc hypste be ge bynad in tohære hyde æt topper hamne. ærest fram aesc hypste to aesc
pyller lace. hanon up to herpade. 7 fram ham herpade sud pihte od hit cymd to gypde hriters popda. 7 fram gypde hriters popda
adun on sreeam to pungyte popdan. hanon pest on hone herpad od ÷ hit cymd to aesc piller lace heapdon.

Acta ÷ hec donatio anno dominice incarnationis dcccc·xxx·vii·

+ Ego adelstanus rex totius bryttannime hoc donum cum signo sce quicis con firmaui.

+ Ego eadmund indolis clito con sensi.   + Ego hopel regulus   + Adelpold   min .
+ Ego pulphelm   sub scripsi.   + Ego pulgar   dux.   + Ælfsic   min .
+ Ego ælpheah,   adquieui.   + Ælphere   dux.   + Pulfsige   min .
+ Ego adelgar   con clusi .   + Ædelstan   dux.   + Odda   min .

18

9 & 10 Two early 'descriptions' of an English village. At the top is a facsimile of an Anglo-Saxon charter dated AD 937 whereby king Athelstan grants his estate of Topsham in Devon to the abbey at Exeter. Most of the landmarks in the charter can be identified precisely today, and look much the same as then. Below is part of the entry about Topsham in Domesday Book (1086), when it had reverted to royal hands. The three estates mentioned here – Pinhoe, Alphington and Topsham are all villages close to Exeter, indeed now absorbed into it as dormitory suburbs.

11 Watendlath (Cumberland), a hamlet of Norse origin, lies by a dark tarn and takes its name from it. *Watend* is the old Norse *Vati-endi*, meaning 'lake end'. Much of the country round here was given to Fountains Abbey as early as 1195, and much of the neighbouring Borrowdale belonged to Furness Abbey, another Cistercian monastery. So the central fells of Cumberland were developed for sheep and cattle ranches from the early thirteenth century onwards. Stonethwaite, in the next valley over the top to the south-west, is another Norse hamlet. 'Thwaite' means a clearing, a common minor place-name in these uplands.

19

12   Blegberry, a fortress-like isolated farmstead which stands just back from the dangerous coast of north-west Devon round Hartland Point. It takes its name ('black *burh*' or fort) from a coastal earthwork which has probably fallen into the turbulent sea. First recorded by name in 1254, it was probably an isolated farm in the royal manor of Hartland at the time of the Norman Conquest. With its wells and springs, it was self-contained and well-nigh impregnable against coastal attack. The farmhouse itself stands in a courtyard behind these walls.

13   The landscape of woodland-clearance: no village anywhere, but isolated farm-steads dotted about, usually at the end of narrow lanes suitable only for tractors and Land Rovers. Note the tiny irregular-shaped fields around some of the older farmsteads, most of which existed before the Norman Conquest. Two ridgeways, probably prehistoric, cross this piece of country, giving the original access to early colonists. They found a water-supply and shelter in the deep combes, and proceeded to hack at the woods all round to create new fields, possibly even burning the trees down to get quicker results.

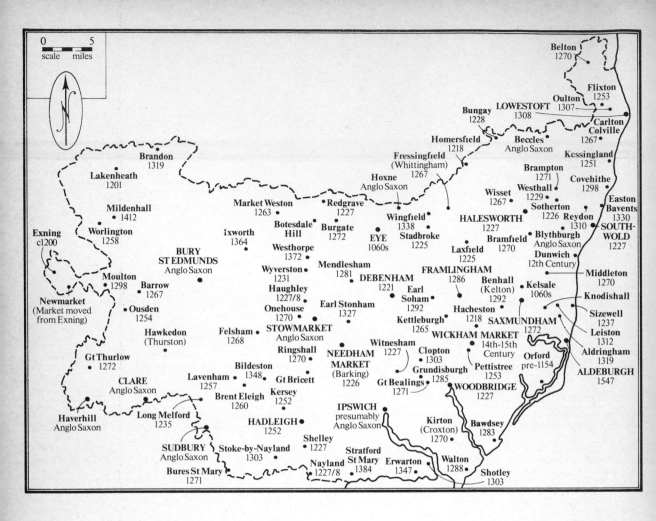

The map shows place names with dates across Suffolk, including:

Belton 1270, Flixton 1253, Oulton 1307, Lowestoft 1308, Bungay 1228, Beccles Anglo Saxon, Carlton Colville 1267, Homersfield 1218, Kessingland 1251, Fressingfield (Whittingham) 1267, Brampton 1271, Covehithe 1298, Hoxne Anglo Saxon, Wisset 1267, Westhall 1229, Easton Bavents, Brandon 1319, Redgrave 1227, Wingfield 1338, Halesworth 1227, Sotherton 1226, Reydon 1310, South-Wold 1227, Lakenheath 1201, Market Weston 1263, Burgate 1272, Eye 1060s, Stadbroke 1225, Bramfield 1270, Blythburgh 1270, Dunwich 12th Century, Mildenhall 1412, Botesdale Hill, Ixworth 1364, Laxfield 1225, Middleton 1270, Exning c1200, Worlington 1258, Westhorpe 1372, Mendlesham 1281, Framlingham 1286, Benhall (Kelton) 1292, Kelsale 1060s, Knodishall, Bury St Edmunds Anglo Saxon, Wyverston 1231, Debenham 1221, Earl Soham 1292, Hacheston 1218, Saxmundham 1272, Sizewell 1237, Moulton 1298, Barrow 1267, Haughley 1227/8, Earl Stonham 1327, Kettleburgh 1265, Wickham Market 14th-15th Century, Leiston 1312, Newmarket (Market moved from Exning), Ousden 1254, Onehouse 1270, Stowmarket Anglo Saxon, Witnesham 1227, Clopton 1303, Pettistree 1253, Orford pre-1154, Aldringham 1319, Hawkedon (Thurston), Felsham 1268, Grundisburgh 1285, Aldeburgh 1547, Gt Thurlow 1272, Ringshall 1270, Needham Market (Barking) 1226, Gt Bealings 1271, Woodbridge 1227, Clare Anglo Saxon, Bildeston, Lavenham 1257, Gt Bricett 1348, Brent Eleigh 1260, Kersey 1252, Ipswich presumably Anglo Saxon, Kirton (Croxton) 1270, Bawdsey 1283, Haverhill Anglo Saxon, Long Melford 1235, Hadleigh 1252, Shelley 1227, Walton 1288, Sudbury Anglo Saxon, Stoke-by-Nayland 1303, Stratford St Mary, Erwarton 1347, Bures St Mary 1271, Nayland 1227/8, Shotley 1303

14   As villages became established, many obtained grants of weekly markets (and sometimes annual fairs) from the lord of the manor. This map, taken from Norman Scarfe's *The Suffolk Landscape*, shows the extraordinary number of markets that existed by medieval times. A dozen markets were already established in Suffolk by 1086. Most were first set up between 1227 and 1310. Aldeburgh got its market as late as 1547, by which date no fewer than 98 towns and villages (about one in five of all places) had a market. Norfolk had as many as 130 such markets at one time. A great number decayed and ceased to exist during the fifteenth century.

THE LANDSCAPE OF COLONISATION

2

After some six or seven hundred years of colonisation since the Romans departed most English villages had come into existence; and in those parts of England where hamlets and isolated farmsteads are typical these too already existed in their thousands. Thus the map of Devon, say, in the eleventh century would have looked very like the Ordnance map of today, with thousands of farm-names dotted all over it, and thousands of miles of lanes joining them (plate 13). Isolated farmsteads on this scale did not result from any breaking-up of an old village: they were an aboriginal form of settlement. A similar pattern would have been found in other parts of the country. There might have been as much land under the plough in 1086 as in the year 1914.

Despite this astonishing fact, our villages, hamlets, and farmsteads were mere islands – large or small – in a great sea of waste. Not that all this was entirely useless, for millions of acres were common pastures that were vital to the farming economy anywhere in England. And rather more than a million acres of common land remain as such to the present day, some of it lowland common like the heaths and commons of the Home Counties, and a good deal of it upland common like the moorlands of the north of England and the west (plate 17).

Although nearly every English village – except those that spawned with the Industrial Revolution – had appeared in the landscape by the time the Norman plunderers took over, many millions of acres remained to be rescued from their natural state and colonised. This vast area was under wood, or scrubby heath, or was stony untouched moorland. Besides the woods and moors, vast areas consisted of marshland, some of it under water for half the year but useful for summer grazing when it dried out. Then there was the Fenland, a different sort of landscape with a distinct kind of history from the marshland. Indeed, the Fenland of eastern England, it has been said, 'presents one of the most completely recognisable ancient landscapes in western Europe'. This remarkable history was not suspected until quite recent times. Finally, there was the unending battle with the sea, which flowed at high tide over acres of land that was potentially valuable for grazing if only it could be rescued and permanently protected.

It is impossible to put a precise date to the period of colonisation which in a sense had been going on since neolithic times in some parts of England. But the tenth century seems as good as any starting-point for a period which lasted without a break until the coming of the Black Death in 1348 eased the growing pressure of population on the land. For some four hundred years then (say 950 to 1350) new farmland was being wrested from the sea, reclaimed from the inland marshes, cleared of woodland cover, and ploughed higher and higher up the moorland slopes.

Probably more land was reclaimed from natural woodland than from any other source, partly because it covered a larger area (except perhaps moorlands, some of which were intractable even to land-hungry medieval farmers) and partly because it was on the whole easier to clear. There is no doubt that both in prehistoric and historic times men cleared large tracts of woodland by the simple process of burning the trees and undergrowth. Several place-names suggest that the initial space for whole villages was created in this way. *Barnet* means 'the place cleared by burning' and *Brentwood* means simply 'burnt wood'. *Swithland* on the edge of Charnwood Forest in Leicestershire is the Scandinavian equivalent, meaning again 'burnt wood'. Wholesale clearance by fire was relatively safe when there was enough land for all, but even by the time of Ine (688–94) it was found necessary to penalise anyone whose fire got out of control and burnt another man's trees. Smaller trees and undergrowth would be cleared by axe and mattock. Hundreds of farm-names of medieval date testify to their origin in woodland country. In East Anglia, on the heavily wooded claylands of mid-Suffolk, isolated farmsteads were moated around (see plate 19). The distribution of moated homesteads in England is very uneven. Thus Essex and Suffolk between them have well over a thousand of these sites; Yorkshire comes next with about 256 and Lincoln and Warwickshire with about 200 each. On the other hand, Cornwall has not a single moated site, and Devon only eleven. It has recently been suggested that this distribution of moated sites is not entirely a matter of soil and geography, but that a moated house might have been regarded as a sort of status symbol in certain localities.

On the high moorlands the great obstacle, apart from a hard climate, was the fact that they were pretty thickly covered with stones, all of which had to be cleared by hand. The medieval peasant farmer must have spent half his time picking stones off the surface and piling them up to form boundary walls – drystone walling, skilfully built without any mortar. Where he came across a huge boulder, too big to move or not worth the effort, he incorporated it in his boundary wall as one can frequently see on the Yorkshire and south-western moorlands. Sometimes an enormous boulder was used as the corner-stone of a peasant house, the starting-point from which two walls were continued. All this was slow work, and the fields so cleared and walled around were usually small – perhaps an acre or less. But in such conditions, with harvest and hay failures only too frequent, every small enclosure, even half an acre, stood between the peasant family and starvation. Under the pressure of population and the need to bring new land into use by colonists from the nearest village or hamlet, cultivation terraces could reach remarkable altitudes, as on Challacombe Common on eastern Dartmoor, where they can be seen at a height of 1500 feet. They were created by family labour (no wage bills) and yielded poor crops of oats. Often, however, a frontier wall (plate 30) was built before the top was reached. Beyond this the moorland was left uncleared, but was used for summer grazing.

Much of this work of clearance was the work of peasant farmers working on their own account, but often there were great capitalist landlords – chiefly the richer monasteries – who cleared tracts of moorland at a time and turned them into sheep and cattle ranches that stretched for miles over the fells. Here and there a small peasant farmhouse appeared in the solitary landscape,

I   Maxey church, in the Welland valley, stands isolated upon a low mound, nearly a mile from its village. The present church is mostly twelfth century in date but the mound on which it stands may well be a prehistoric burial mound of some religious significance. If so, it is a site of tremendous continuity. Large-scale excavations for gravel all round this area show that the dry, slightly elevated land has been occupied on and off since neolithic times. Near the church a buried field-pattern of Iron Age and Roman date has been discovered, and not far away a Dark Age village has been located. So the first church was formerly close to the original village. (Chapter 5)

II Heath Chapel lies high up in the Clee Hills of Shropshire, a daughter foundation of the mother-church of Stoke St Milborough. Its name betrays its origin as a late colonisation of the heathland. A new community had come into being and this perfect little Norman church (c. 1150) set the seal upon it, though it never achieved the full status of a parish church. The village was deserted long ago, but in the surrounding fields (at the right time of the year) may be traced the extensive earthworks that represent the old house-sites and lanes. These are best seen behind the chapel. (Chapter 4)

III   Linton, founded beside a small stream flowing into Wharfedale, is in stone country—mostly Mountain Limestone. The earliest Anglian settlement (perhaps eighth century) and its first enclosures from the waste, were surrounded by a high stone wall. It is dry-stone walling upon a base some four or five feet thick. Some of the wall shown here probably dates from the earliest settlement, though it has naturally been repaired at intervals since. Later stages in the expansion of the village fields can be traced in other walls round about, and on the map. (Chapter 1)

IV Bury Barton in mid-Devon is recorded by name in Domesday Book, but as it stands tucked inside a civilian earthwork of Iron Age or Roman date it has probably been farmed continuously since that time. The farmstead lies off the picture to the right. The never-failing pond, fed secretly from below, is the *fons et origo* of this ancient site. The isolation of the farmstead accounts for its possessing its own little chapel, shown here. It was licensed by the bishop in 1434. *Bury* refers to the earthwork (*burh*), while *Barton* is the common South-Western word for the demesne farm of the manor—the lord's farm. (Chapter 1)

V   The hill pastures of the Pennines, above all the sweet grass of the Mountain Limestone country, fed vast flocks of sheep from monastic days onwards. Most of the monasteries in the surrounding lowlands had great sheep-ranches up here (see back cover), which necessitated driving the animals (*droving*) for miles along tracks that often came into existence for this purpose, though some are older. Though mostly deserted now, except for ramblers, they can be traced for miles to the nearest market-town or sheep-fair. Mastiles Lane, near Malham, is one of the best preserved of such wide and ancient drove-rods. (Chapter 8)

VI   West Shropshire was one of the richest lead-mining areas in Britain. Here at Snailbeach is the extraordinary scene—for a rural landscape—created by lead-mining from Roman times down to within living memory. These mountains of waste look like snow-clad hills when seen from miles away. Derelict mine-buildings and disused railway tracks and sheds complete the scene. Though at first sight a huge blot upon the country landscape, this relic might well be considered now for preservation as an Ancient Monument of early mining. (Chapter 9)

VII   Quebec Farm, in the airy Leicestershire pastures, gives itself away by its name,
         commemorating as it does Wolfe's victory in Canada in 1759. The parish of
         Sileby, in which it lies, was enclosed by parliamentary act in 1760 and its lands
         re-allotted. The richer farmers could afford to build handsome houses like this
         one in the middle of their new farms: a typical mid-Georgian house in the
         Midland style. Not far away are Hanover Farm and Belle Isle, both redolent of
         the same era. (Chapter 7)

VIII Although there was a bridge at Hebden Bridge in medieval times, and a few houses survive here and there from the pre-industrial age, the town really originated with the development of water-power in the late eighteenth century, which brought cotton and woollen mills into the valley-bottom. The opening of the Rochdale Canal in 1798 gave an immense impetus to the new town, especially when (in 1804) it became the first canal to cross the Pennines. Traffic on the canal reached its peak in the 1880s, and it was closed only in 1952. (Chapter 9)

the home of the stockman with a tiny network of stone-walled enclosures around it, for a few necessary crops and for shelter for stock in winter. On these moorlands, especially the lands once owned by Fountains and other great Yorkshire abbeys, and above all on the sweet pastures of the Mountain Limestone, you can still stand in a purely medieval landscape: the only sounds are those of the wailing lapwing, or the long trilling of curlews, and the cry of distant sheep. Nothing has changed since the twelfth or thirteenth century. Such a landscape can best be seen to the north-east of Malham Tarn, and to the east of the great flanks of Fountains Fell which bears to this day the name of the mountain pastures that once belonged to that beautiful abbey far away in its sheltered lowland.

In quite another sort of country, land was being reclaimed from that ancient enemy the sea, above all along the east coast. Here at low tides, miles of potentially good salt-marsh was exposed. 'Sea-banks' were being constructed from at least the tenth century, part of a communal effort by several villages, so that the high tides were shut out for good. The land so rescued was left to dry out, to form salt marshes; then after a period it was brought into permanent use for cattle grazing. Later, when fully dried out, it formed rich arable land.

The coastal marshlands of England have a complicated history. A whole book could be written about them alone. They still have their special lovers, a class apart from those who seek solitude in the perhaps more obvious beauty of the high moorlands. It takes time to appreciate the special quality of a marshland landscape, with its towering skies, the smell of the sea behind the retaining banks, the wild birds that frequent the lonely miles especially in winter.

The marshland is quite different from the Fens. It was on the Lincolnshire marshlands where Mablethorpe now sprawls that Tennyson as a boy saw

> Stretch'd wide and wild the waste enormous marsh,
> Where from the frequent bridge,
> Like emblems of infinity,
> The trenchèd waters run from sky to sky.

One's heart bleeds for the people who live on Foulness, or those to whom it is a place in which to recapture their souls, when it is discussed as a place to be covered with concrete and noise. On Foulness – 'the headland of the wild birds' – some embanking against the sea had probably begun before the Norman Conquest and certainly by the twelfth century. It was a long piecemeal process, some banks and ditches being constructed as late as the fifteenth century.

Around the shores of the Wash, too, especially on the west and southern sides, there is a long history of embanking against the sea, though the so-called 'Roman Bank' marked on the maps is most likely of tenth-century date. Romney Marsh in Kent has a history possibly going back to Roman times. Certainly Anglo-Saxon charters and Domesday Book show most of its villages already in existence. Ivychurch, for example, occurs as a name in the eleventh century, suggesting a church already ancient.

Inland, too, the large-scale work of reclaiming marshes such as the Somerset

Levels was the work of the opulent abbeys – Glastonbury, Athelney, and Muchelney – which had been endowed with these swampy wastes at least as early as the eighth century. Work was certainly going on here in the tenth century. It is rarely that we hear any name of the countless millions of people, peasants as well as bigger men, who created this kind of landscape and turned it into rich pastures; but we learn from Domesday Book that Glastonbury was then employing a drainage engineer – Girard Fossarius – probably a skilled man of foreign origin (from the Low Countries?) who was probably brought in by a Norman abbot. In a few years he had succeeded, by means of banks and ditches, in multiplying the value of the abbey lands in the marshes by about four – a tremendous achievement.

Both marshland and fenland, two distinct landscapes, were in fact already old landscapes before the great revival of drainage schemes in the tenth century. Foulness, for example, is rich in Romano-British remains, and the Somerset Levels have produced brushwood causeways dating from neolithic times. At Westhay near Glastonbury a figurine was found in the deep peat which has been dated to between 2700 and 2000 BC. The history of these landscapes, both fen and marsh, has been immensely complicated by the advance and recession of the sea at different periods. Old landscapes disappeared under silt and peat, and a fresh start had to be made in late Saxon times, most of it by organised communal effort and in a piecemeal fashion, just like the piecemeal reclamation of moorland from its native stone. Every field, whether arable or pasture or salt marsh, was another step away from starvation.

The colonisation of medieval England, filling in the empty spaces so to speak, went on apace during the twelfth and thirteenth centuries: the work of rich and famous abbeys and of a multitude of peasant families whose names are nowhere recorded. Then came the retreat from the marginal lands with the hammer-blows of the Black Death and the phenomenon of deserted villages (see chapter 4) but not every landscape was equally affected. The great sheep and cattle ranches of Northern England required little labour and were never abandoned. We see them today almost as a medieval peasant would have seen them, watching the cloud-shadows flowing over the lovely sides of Fountains Fell and Ingleborough and Penyghent.

Besides the major kinds of landscape – the woodland clearances, the sea-banks, the winding ditches of the inner marshlands, the lonely stone-built farmsteads on the high moors – there were two very special landscapes, with a history all of their own such as the Breckland (plates 24 and 25) and the Norfolk Broads (plate 21). Few parts of England are without these small-scale enclaves with their own devotees who will not tell their secrets.

15   Staverton Park, in east Suffolk, is one of the rare fragments left in England of an untouched natural landscape. Eleven main types of vegetation have been recognised, but the predominant impression (especially in the part known as the Thicks) is one of decaying tangled oaks and ancient holly trees. It survived in its natural state because it was set aside as a hunting-park sometime in the thirteenth century, its open glades first used as a pasture for deer, and it has never been cleared.

16   Wicken Fen in Cambridgeshire has every appearance of a natural landscape of fenland; but the whole fenland was fairly thickly settled in Romano-British times and many of the 'droves' (like Sedger's Drove, shown here) are of Roman origin. Fodderfen Drove near by has produced Roman burial urns. Drainage was a perpetual problem, and some settled areas were abandoned for good, probably early in the fifth century, when the elaborate administrative organisation was destroyed. Wicken Fen reverted to an overgrown and water-logged landscape and now belongs to the National Trust.

17   Bodmin Moor in Cornwall, showing the granite tor of Brown Willy and the 'frontier wall' which marked the limit of medieval colonisation. Beyond this massive earthen bank, faced with stone gathered from the moorland surface – hence the local word of 'moorstone' for granite – lies the uncolonised common pastures where no farms were created. Fernacre Farm, not far away, recorded first in 1327, is now deserted. Garrow, in the same area, has been excavated and is worth visiting. These high moorlands were colonised during the population-pressure of the thirteenth century.

18   Lower Tor Farm, on Dartmoor, showing a typical 'long house' of basically
      medieval construction. There was a common entrance for cattle and men, the
      former turning left in the passage into the shippon or byre, the family turning
      right into the domestic rooms. Lower Tor is first recorded by name in a
      document dated 1249. Though this house was modernised c. 1600, it retains
      clear traces to the expert eye of an original medieval open hall. Many such
      long-houses are to be found on and around Dartmoor, the visible signs of the
      colonisation of the moorland.

19   There are over five hundred moated sites in Suffolk alone, mostly on the heavy boulder clays of the central 'uplands'. Most of these farms were cleared from the dense woodlands and moated around from the beginning – partly for drainage on the heavy soils, partly for a fish-supply, and partly perhaps for defence in such isolated places. Parham Old Hall (or Moat Hall) is a wonderful survival of c. 1500, in elaborate brickwork. Even so, this house probably replaced one of twelfth or thirteenth-century date, when many of these moated homesteads were first created.

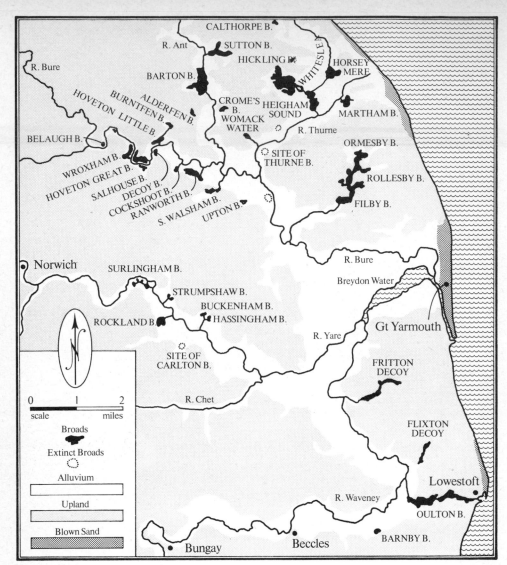

20   The origin of the Norfolk Broads was for long a subject for speculation, one theory being that they had resulted from a marine transgression in comparatively recent times. A combined attack by experts in the 1950s demonstrated conclusively that they were the result of deep peat-cutting in the medieval period over some 400 years. Peat was a valuable fuel in a basically treeless region. Later, water-seepage caused the abandonment of peat-cutting: marshes developed, and finally enough water came in to create these artificial 'lakes'.

21   Ranworth Broad, near the river Bure, is first recorded in 1275 when the tithes of a 'turbary' (turf or peat) were given to a local monastery, but it may have existed a century before as several turbaries are recorded by the second half of the twelfth century. The vegetation of this landscape is typical: so are the two windmills. The slow rivers of East Anglia produced few water-mills but the persistent wind over the levels gave rise to windmills from about 1200 on.

22   A characteristic piece of marshland in the Somerset Levels, reclaimed by Glastonbury Abbey which owned vast estates in central Somerset. The narrow and curving ditch (or *rhine*, the local word) is typical of early drainage channels, and the willows or osiers are the most familiar tree nowadays. The church of Othery (with its village hidden) stands on a low island, perhaps twenty or thirty feet above the original marshes, but sufficiently high to be free from flooding at any time. Othery church was largely rebuilt by the abbey out of its large revenues, as were Weston Zoyland and other churches on its estates: all just before the great plunderer Henry VIII put an end to it all.

23   The Cistercian Abbey of Fountains, founded in the closing days of December 1132 by the banks of the river Skell, is one of the loveliest monastic ruins in Europe. It is named after the six springs which break forth here. Endowed with great estates almost from the first, it was one of the great colonising agents of medieval England, above all in the uplands of Craven in West Yorkshire where the abbey is said to have possessed a hundred square miles of land (some 60,000 acres) within one ring fence. By Henry VIII's time it was one of the richest abbeys in England and a special prize for that deadly predator.

24 & 25 The Breckland overlaps north-west Suffolk and south-west Norfolk. It is largely a sandy heath, the driest and most arid part of the British Isles; but before the new pattern of forestry and airfields emerged it was one of the most fascinating of all our heathland landscapes. Most of its villages lie in the river valleys or on the edge of the fen. But under the population-pressure of the twelfth and thirteenth centuries the heath itself was colonised, using the *meres* (like Langmere above) for water. A score of such villages were later abandoned, or have shrunk to a church and a hall-farm, for it was always marginal land. The scene round Langmere shows the more natural landscape: that below (near Cockley Cley) an arable landscape dying away into a modern forest.

BOUNDARIES IN THE LANDSCAPE

3

Boundaries are one of the most permanent and ancient features in the English landscape. They are monuments to the long and unbroken continuity of life in this country, at least until recent years when German bombers and English town councils between them obliterated the age-long pattern of our town-plans; and modern excavating and earth-moving machinery has wiped out major earthworks (hedges, banks, and ditches) in the countryside which earlier men had failed to move even had they wished to. But before modern man came along with his implements of destruction, a physical boundary tended to be taken over century after century, age after age, because it was already there, and because it represented physical evidence of decisions made long ago and fixed solidly on the ground – a Romano-British estate, a Saxon overlord's private estate, a medieval farm, a field.

There were even towns where, despite the inevitable changes of centuries, the boundary walls of houses and shops remained unchanged, for seven or eight hundred years as in Canterbury or Chelmsford and probably countless other towns which were never properly studied before the acids of modernity dissolved them. In the countryside some of these ancient boundaries still stand out bold and clear, once we have learnt to recognise them for what they are, like the Old Hundred Lane in mid-Suffolk (plate 26); but in other places they are hidden from sight until the skilled historian, aided by the archaeologist, lays bare the immense continuity of village field-boundaries as at Great Wymondley in Hertfordshire. Here the Roman pattern of centuriation survived vestigially in the open-field pattern of fields at the beginning of the nineteenth century and the village itself stands on the site of the British village once attached to the villa of some great man's estate. Or to move to East Anglia, the surviving pattern of by-roads, lanes, and hedges at Holme-next-the-Sea in Norfolk still clearly marks the field-pattern defined in Roman times (see W. G. Hoskins, *Fieldwork in Local History*, pp. 140–2). We no longer believe uncritically that Romano-British landscapes, and perhaps even older ones, were obliterated by fresh military conquests, and new landscapes created. The new men took over as landlords but farming still had to go on. It was a matter of life and death that the annual harvest should be gathered in, whatever was happening at the landlord level. Natural disasters have probably done more to destroy the continuity of the landscape in many parts of England than any fire-and-sword mentality.

It is likely that the oldest boundaries were merely ditches, especially on gravelly and medium-loam soils, and these have disappeared except from aerial photographs and the archaeologist's trowel. These ditches were also used for drainage, as they were in the medieval marshland of the Somerset Levels and are down to this day. In the stony moorlands of the West, however, roughly-made drystone walling was used from the Bronze Age onwards. Certainly there are many Early Iron Age field-walls surviving in the uplands of the Land's End peninsula (plate 28).

The larger Romano-British villas must have had defined boundaries but we are only just beginning to recognise them on the ground. The Roman villa at Ditchley in Oxfordshire comprised some 875 acres and its boundaries have been worked out with a fair degree of certainty. Ancient woodland formed most of its perimeter, but the earthwork still known as Grim's Dyke filled in the gaps. This earthwork, which is not continuous, was thrown up shortly before the middle of the first century AD. What is fascinating, too, is that nearly the whole of the villa boundaries were taken over much later as parish boundaries, which indicates an estate or unit clearly recognisable in late Saxon times. Whether such evidence is good enough to assume unbroken continuity of farming from Roman times to the present day is still a matter of opinion; but I myself believe that the case is good enough, if only for the simple and fundamental reason that every harvest was a gamble. The villa buildings might be allowed to fall into ruin, like so many country houses in our own age, but the farms on the estate went on.

Wars and conquests left most of England undisturbed. A few areas might be ravaged by some military fanatic, and the unpaid soldiers of the English Civil War, left to their own devices, might burn and pillage, but it was all very local and Nature's wounds soon healed. See how on many an English chancel wall a monument of Charles II's time refers to those unhappy days merely as 'the Late Troubles'. Most landscapes were only superficially scratched until the large-scale devastation of the Industrial Revolution in the late eighteenth century and the early nineteenth. In other parts we can discern layer beneath layer: everything is older than we think.

At Ditchley (Oxon) the villa boundaries were taken over for later uses. So it was, I think, in mid-Suffolk where the Old Hundred Lane looks suspiciously like the northern rampart of a large villa-estate centred upon Stonham, some two miles away. The parish to the right of the bank in plate 26 is called Mickfield, meaning 'the big field'. This is how the Old English saw it when they moved in, a large already-cleared area which they took over. And what else could it have been but a Romano-British estate in recognisable shape? When the administrative unit of the hundred was created a thousand years later, there was not the slightest necessity to remove this massive rampart and make a new boundary somewhere else.

Apart from villa estates and large native farms, it was usually sufficient – in a countryside where there was plenty of room for all – to define territories by reference to natural features in an untamed landscape: the edge of a forest, some big river, a great marsh that acted as a barrier. But as the countryside filled up, the old vague natural boundaries had to be supplemented by artificial earthworks. In the earliest Anglo-Saxon grants of land the boundaries are still rather vaguely defined in relation to a river or a forest, but by the ninth century it had become necessary to define the bounds much more precisely. Depending upon the area covered, and even a small estate granted by charter might be ten miles around, a dozen or a score of landmarks might be named. Some have perished long ago, such as a particular tree or a stone, but many survive and may be recognised for what they are (plates 27 and 28).

The number of land-grants that survive from Old English times is comparatively small. In Devon and Cornwall alone there are something like a hundred but not all give detailed boundaries (plate 9). In parts of Eastern England, however, overrun by the Danes, very few survive. Yet it is likely that though the documentary evidence was destroyed in a Danish raid on some Fenland monastery (these were very big landowners) the physical evidence may well lie there still, awaiting the discerning eye.

Often it is a particularly overgrown and massive hedgebank which betrays the boundary of an Old English estate even when no document survives to say so specifically (plate 29), above all if such a hedgebank is followed for a long distance by parish boundaries. Other ancient hedgebanks may be medieval in date, constructed to define a hunting-park and to keep the wild animals inside the pale. These boundaries can usually be fairly precisely dated, as it was a status symbol to possess such a private hunting-park and required a licence from the King. Hundreds of these licences have been printed from the public records. The technique for recognising these park boundaries on the ground, and for reconstructing their total perimeter, has been worked out by the late O. G. S. Crawford in *Archaeology in the Field*.

So far I have spoken mainly about the boundaries of larger units such as estates and parks, but the unit of cultivation was, of course, the farm. This had its own boundaries; and within the farm there were fields, either walled around or bounded by massive earthen banks as in south-western England. The boundaries of a farm, in the kind of landscape where the typical settlement was the isolated homestead, are often of great antiquity as we now know that thousands of these farms already existed at the time of the Norman Conquest. Often the farm-boundaries are narrow lanes, which perhaps started life as deep ditches: hence the intricate pattern of winding lanes in the west of England. Many run from one farmhouse to another; but many run around the farm and are in fact its ancient boundary.

The mileage of hedges in a county like Devon, where until recent years the fields were small, was enormous. Back in 1844 a surveyor calculated that the hedges in ten parishes in east Devon totalled 1,651 miles – 'half as long again as the Great Wall of China'. One large parish alone had a mileage of hedges that would have stretched in a straight line from Land's End to Edinburgh. Hedgebanks are therefore a marvellous subject for study as boundaries. In recent years Dr Max Hooper of the Nature Conservancy has evolved a technique for estimating the date of hedges by counting the number of different species of shrub in sample lengths, his hypothesis (tested in many parts of England) being that for every different species we can reckon a hundred years of life; so that a hedgebank which produced ten different species could be reckoned to be 1,000 years old, plus or minus 50. This is a highly simplified statement, but in general it works. For a fuller discussion of this remarkable tool for landscape-history, see Dr Hooper's essay in *Hedges and Local History*.

Hedges have been constructed at different periods in different parts of the country. Basically, the hedges of the west are old, some of them aboriginal vestiges of the waste; whereas in those parts of England affected by parliamen-

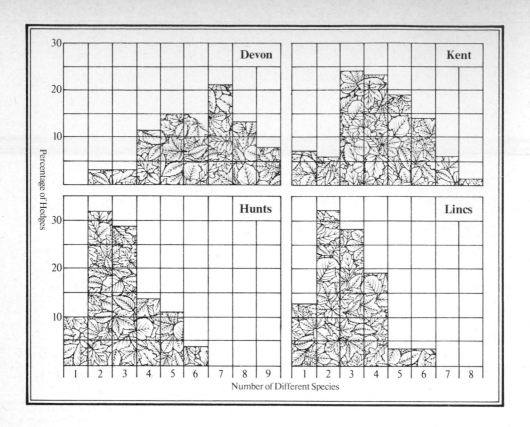

Percentage of Hedges

Number of Different Species

tary enclosure (see chapter 7) a high proportion of the existing hedges are relatively modern. Hence we get very different pictures from different counties if we plot the data about hedge-dating as Dr Hooper has done here. Both Devon and Kent show a high proportion of hedges many centuries old; whereas Lincolnshire and Huntingdonshire show a much higher proportion of 'young' hedges. Even so, when we get down to details in any county, we find examples of all ages. Even in parts of the Midlands we can pass through five centuries of landscape-history in a walk of half a dozen miles.

A great deal of this evidence is now being destroyed with the object of making fields big enough for large-scale cultivation. The arable east of England, especially Suffolk and Norfolk, is suffering cruelly at the hands of the 'barley barons' who mine the soil of its wealth and will eventually leave it worn out. Dr Hooper has estimated that we may have lost a third of our hedges in recent years; in some parts almost seventy per cent has gone. We are not only destroying wild life of all kinds – England will no longer be a nest of singing birds as it once was – but destroying the topsoil which blows about like the American Dustbowl in high winds; but we are losing also irreplaceable evidence for the history of the landscape. Perhaps we can take some historical comfort from the fact that the modern farmer-baron is recreating the landscape of a Romano-British estate – 'the big field' of Mickfield – or the open fields of the medieval Midlands. The historian must always take the long view beyond the immediate destruction.

26   The most spectacular boundary in East Anglia is that dividing Bosmere and Hartismere hundreds in mid-Suffolk. Known for miles as the Old Hundred Lane, it crosses the Roman road (now A140) and is best seen just south of Brockford House (O.S. sheet 136, ref. 119628). It is a wide green trackway with deep ditches on either side. A good deal of it has now been destroyed, but what survives (as shown here) should be scheduled as an Ancient Monument forthwith. It dates certainly from the early tenth century, and may be the northern boundary of a large Romano-British estate centred on Stonham Aspal.

27 & 28   Two ancient boundaries: Above, part of an Anglo-Saxon boundary in Devon
made c. 670 AD when the king gave an estate to Exeter abbey. Here the
boundary is making a big curve which is specifically referred to in the charter
setting out the various landmarks. Below, a wall of large granite boulders
cleared from the moorland of West Penwith in Cornwall. At Boswednack,
nearby, is a network of terraced fields made in the Iron Age and walled in
this way.

29   An untouched, overgrown hedge – actually a double hedgebank with a tangled
pathway between – in the depths of Devon. It is followed by parish boundaries
for some miles, a sure sign of its antiquity as it must have existed when
parishes were first demarcated. In all probability it was originally part of the
boundary of an early Saxon estate (say 650–700 AD). A shrub-count of its more
overgrown stretches would help to settle this point.

30   Limestone walls on Malham Moor in west Yorkshire. The lower walls in the
scene are the older, enclosing small pasture-fields. The former frontier between
cultivation and moor runs straight across the middle of the scene. Rising from it,
and climbing to the summit of the moor, is a magnificent wall made in 1845
when the upper commons were split up and allocated between the different
farms. Note how the later wall climbs from cliff to cliff, using each face as a
natural boundary.

The Old English settlers had a very good eye for viable sites for their settlements, doubtless judging the quality of various soils from an expert knowledge of vegetation. But they seem occasionally to have made mistakes and to have abandoned some sites at a fairly early date; or there may have been some local catastrophe not worthy of record in any national annals. Archaeologists are now turning up a few such sites, like West Stow in Suffolk which was occupied as early as 400 AD and abandoned after some 250 years. No fewer than sixty hut-sites have been unearthed here, all from this period of eight to ten human generations. The likeliest theory for its abandonment is that a better site presented itself about a mile upstream where the present (medieval) village now stands: certainly it ended abruptly but not violently. It is certain that many such peaceful desertions remain to be discovered, and most will appear only by chance as there are usually no surface indications.

The distribution-map (plate 31) records no fewer than 2,263 known sites of deserted villages in England alone. Bearing in mind that some counties have produced not a single site, such as Lancashire and Middlesex, and others are clearly awaiting systematic exploration, such as Suffolk and several others, the final total – if it is ever arrived at – is likely to be well over three thousand 'lost villages'.

A number of well-established villages disappeared as a deliberate policy of monastic houses in the twelfth century. The Cistercians above all sought a solitude and achieved it at times by removing all the inhabitants of an old village to a new place. The monks of Rufford in Nottinghamshire (founded c.1145) destroyed two villages and probably created a new village at Wellow to take the displaced peasants; and the founding of Byland abbey in Yorkshire involved what a modern developer would call 'clearing the site'. Such monastic depopulations may be found in many places in eastern England. A few villages may have perished in wars, though in such cases, and after devastating epidemics, a site was frequently reoccupied as it was too good to lose for ever.

The Black Death, which first struck England in the summer of 1348, and came back repeatedly and in force during the rest of the century, is often thought to have been a prime cause of total abandonment, but such examples are few. Usually there were a few survivors, and even with total mortality a site could be taken up again slowly by people from elsewhere.

Few villages disappeared dramatically as a result of the Black Death, though some such sites are known like Tilgarsley in Oxfordshire. Far more disappeared by a process of slow attrition over generations. Repeated visitations of bubonic plague reduced the population of England by perhaps a half, and in thousands of villages there came a time when there were too few people to carry on the immemorial system of open-field farming. It was then, very often, that a rapacious Tudor squire dealt the final blow and evicted the survivors in order to make room for his extensive sheep and cattle pastures.

Less labour was required to run these wide pastures: often a single shepherd's hut sufficed.

Very few of these abandoned villages have been professionally excavated. For one thing, they are so big and expensive to uncover. Two good examples of large-scale excavation, however, are Wharram Percy on the chalk of the Yorkshire Wolds and Hound Tor, high up on the Dartmoor granite.

Archaeologists are now working on the site of Holyoak, on the borders of Leicestershire and Rutland, and here a complicated story is being unfolded. It is much more complex than the simple statement in a document that tells us that Sir Robert Brudenell, the squire, evicted thirty people from their small arable farms to make way for his cattle and sheep pastures. The record ends: 'They have departed thence and are either idle or have perished.' Other such records tell us that villagers left their farms in tears, and probably went to swell the ranks of homeless vagrants. Already the work at Holyoak has shown that the site was occupied over an astonishing period, and it is reckoned that there may be some two hundred house-sites in all, not just the five or six farmsteads that reaped their last harvest in the autumn of 1496.

Whereas some villages were finished off at a stroke, others took longer to die. Great Stretton, in Leicestershire also, took some five generations to die. Today it is just a church in a field by itself, but to the south of it is a tumbled piece of ground which at first sight seems quite without plan. In fact it consists of a fairly regular pattern of grass-covered platforms with gullies or little lanes running between them. The platforms are the sites of medieval peasant houses. Since these were built of mud and timber they have perished completely (unlike the granite walls at Hound Tor) and all we see is the foundation platforms of rubble masonry, now deep in grass. At the bottom of the field is the rectangular moated site where the medieval squire once lived. The best time of year to see these sites is early spring or winter before the growing grass conceals the evidence.

At one time Great Stretton had some fifteen to twenty farmhouses and cottages inside this field. But one of the long themes of English history is that the land has tended to fall into fewer and fewer hands. It is a process that has been reversed in the past forty years through wars and heavy taxation but for a thousand years or more it was otherwise. By Charles II's time there were only five farmers left instead of fifteen, and the land had all gone over to pasture. The big men know the use to which land can most profitably be put, and in Leicestershire this was sheep and cattle pastures. The small men disappear. So Great Stretton died slowly over a space of four or five generations and is now a melancholy place to visit on a winter's afternoon: a touching little bit of English history.

The marked concentration of deserted village sites in the eastern half of England is partly due to the fact that the village was the more typical form of settlement on this side of the country. It is easier to rediscover a village site, which may cover several acres and present obvious signs on the ground, than to find a lost hamlet on the western side. Even with aerial photography this is not easy.

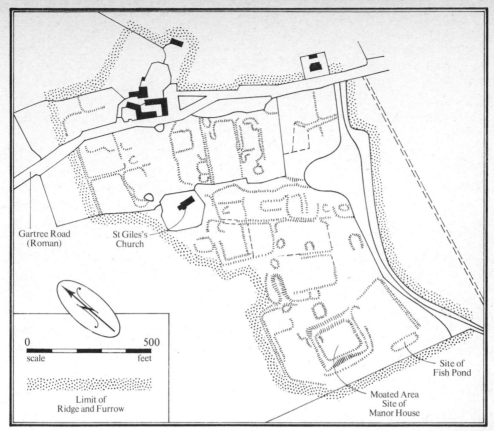

Gartree Road (Roman)

St Giles's Church

0   500

scale   feet

Limit of
Ridge and Furrow

Site of
Fish Pond

Moated Area
Site of
Manor House

Great Stretton

Apart from the early kinds of desertion already mentioned, the great majority took place in the period of roughly 1450–1600. A great number of villages had already been deserted when the government woke up to the fact and passed its first act against the depopulation of villages in 1489. For various reasons these acts proved ineffective.

Other desertions took place at later dates, principally of mining villages when the ores gave out, as up near the top of the Stiperstones in Shropshire. Here the lead-mining petered out early in this century, the small farming crofts were not enough to sustain a living, and the families of Blackmoregate drifted away one by one. It is an isolated site, and well worth visiting. The sites of deserted villages worth visiting are set out in a recent work by M. W. Beresford and J. G. Hurst on *Deserted Medieval Villages* but the man who knows his own locality well will be able to find his own sites with the aid of the one-inch Ordnance map. When one has seen a good site, the signs on other sites become unmistakeable.

Villages and hamlets were not the only kinds of settlement to fail. There are scores of failed towns. Their history is, however, entirely different. Lydford, in Devon on the western edge of Dartmoor, was a Saxon borough founded as a military fortress against the Danes in the ninth century. Under the Normans, strong castles were built at Okehampton and Launceston, and Lydford ceased to have any value. Nor had it any valuable hinterland from which to draw trade, so it began to decay as early as the twelfth century. Apart from its one main street, one can still see the grassy side-lanes that represented the minor streets of the Saxon town.

It was the twelfth and thirteenth centuries, however, that saw what has been called 'the fever of borough creation'. Most of these were optimistic speculations by lords of rural manors who foresaw urban rents and market and fair tolls arising from some corner of their estates instead of just farm-rents. Some of these speculations came off. Thus the A30, the spinal road of the south-west until recently, attracted settlers to its side, and down this road a string of little towns grew between about 1190 and 1250 – notably Crewkerne and Chard in Somerset, and Honiton and Okehampton in Devon. These are still busy little towns, but South Zeal (plate 37) on the same trunk-route failed to come off. So did several of the Cornish boroughs like Mitchell, or Grampound and Tregony not far away. Most of these Cornish speculations failed to grow into true towns despite their borough charters, but acquired a new kind of life, if one can call it that, by being chosen to be parliamentary boroughs under the Tudors anxious to pack the House of Commons. In this way Cornwall returned no fewer than forty-four members to the Commons. Some of them were notorious even among the 'pocket boroughs' but at least they sometimes returned some remarkable men to the House at an early age without a tiresome struggle.

Devon had more than seventy 'boroughs' in medieval times, about half of which failed to survive. Some are now represented by little backwoods villages, like Rackenford in mid-Devon, but few do not reveal traces of their urban beginnings to those who know how to recognise them, such as the sudden widening of the main street where the weekly market was held six hundred or so years ago, or the bit of common land on the edge of the village which was once enlivened by the annual fair. One of the most revealing of these little failed towns is Montacute in Somerset where the abbot of Cluny had his markets and fairs and created a borough as early as the eleventh century. But the facts of geography were against it – the main cause of the failure of most of these speculations. Either they were too near to a better-sited and older town, or they had no hinterland on which to draw for trade. So at Montacute one sees the large open square in the middle with the nameplate conspicuously placed – *The Borough* – but it is now, as so often, a handy car park and no more.

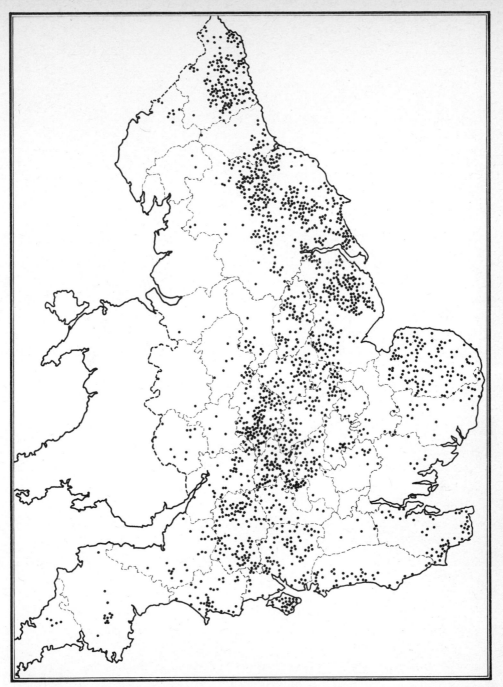

31 This map of the distribution of deserted medieval villages shows all those
known up to the end of the year 1968. In all, no fewer than 2,263 sites are now
known, but many more await discovery. The inevitable gaps in such a map are
discussed on page 45. Thus the Staffordshire total of 22 sites (in 1962) will
almost certainly rise to over 100 when the necessary exploration has been done,
but the basic concentration of deserted villages in the lowland zone of eastern
England and the Midlands is unlikely to be significantly changed.

32   Ingarsby, in the uplands of east Leicestershire, is one of the best-preserved sites of 'lost villages'. The manor belonged entirely to Leicester Abbey, who in 1469 enclosed it all with hedges and ditches and converted it to sheep and cattle pastures. The few remaining open-field arable farmers were driven out, and all one sees now are the rectangular mounds that mark their house-sites and the 'hollow ways' that show where the village streets and lanes ran. The scene today is still completely medieval; aged and twisted thorn trees and cattle grazing over the rich grasslands.

33   South Middleton in Northumberland is another fine example of a deserted village site, not least because the pattern of 'ridge and furrow' – the former arable lands – is so strikingly preserved, right up to the edge of the former village. Here the rectangular platforms of the house-sites of the peasant farmers also stand out sharply. Northumberland has no fewer than 165 such 'lost villages', the result of the conversion of arable to cattle and sheep pastures by big landlords. Much of this desertion took place later than in the Midlands, a great deal of it in the Elizabethan period.

34   Egmere stands in a lonely part of north Norfolk. The village decayed during the fifteenth century. All that is left is Egmere Farm, some ruined cottages, and mounds representing former house-sites. The church was unroofed for its lead, the walls partly pulled down, in Henry VIII's time. Today all that is left is the early fourteenth-century tower and fragments of walls. Not far away (see sheet 125 of the one-inch map) are the remains of Quarles church, already in ruins by the 1560s. The old village lies under the plantation just west of the church. The ruined church of Waterden (only the Hall and a house are left of the village) lies W.S.W. of Egmere — three melancholy ruins in one small piece of country.

35   Torksey was once a considerable town on the Trent, important for its river traffic even in Saxon times. It was a transhipment point for Lincoln, which was reached by the Foss Dyke (seen crossing the picture from left to right). Thanks to this canal, first made by the Romans, Yorkshire and the Midlands were linked to Boston on the Wash. The town of Torksey, now shrunk to the village (near top-centre), occupied the whole of the two fields down to the Foss Dyke and had extensive wharves along its banks. It decayed slowly from the late fourteenth century onwards.

36   The Normans introduced castles into the English landscape. In Cornwall only two are recorded in Domesday Book, one at Launceston, the other at Trematon. Both were built by the Count of Mortain, lord of Cornwall. Trematon guarded an inlet off the vital estuary of the Tamar. In both cases the Count set up a market below his castle, both 'removed' from earlier monastic markets and planted where the great man wanted them. A market usually marked the beginning of a town, but whereas Launceston took root and flourished, Trematon failed to come off, though it was called a 'borough' for long afterwards.

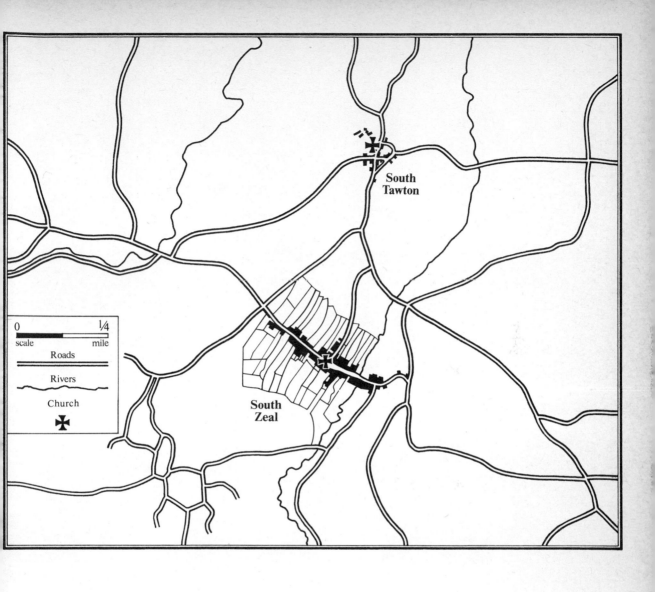

37   South Zeal in Devon lay on the great medieval road from London to Land's
      End (roughly the present A30, though the village is now by-passed). It is first
      recorded in 1167, when the road had attracted perhaps an inn, a smithy and a
      few houses from the mother-village of South Tawton. By 1299 there must have
      been enough growth to encourage the lord of South Tawton to grant a weekly
      market and two annual fairs to Zeal as a hopeful speculation. It received a
      borough charter and was laid out on a regular plan, still well-evidenced to this
      day. The widening of the street where the chapel now stands represents
      the medieval market place. But it all failed.   55

38   Hedon, in the East Riding, grew up near the mother village of Preston, with
access to the important estuary of the Humber. It started on a low heathy
eminence (Hedon ='heath hill') early in the twelfth century and flourished
until it had three churches and wharves along three havens. Its streets were
regularly planned, crossing each other at right angles, and the whole burghal
area of 320 acres lay within the 'town ditch'. Only one church remains, but the
original street-plan and the grass-grown havens can still be traced. The town
decayed largely in the fifteenth century, outclassed as a port by nearby Hull.

The parish churches of England are its glory and distinction, something one only completely realises when travelling through Europe until one reaches, perhaps, the staggering beauty of the Baroque and Rococo in southern Germany and beyond, so utterly different from anything we have (except milder examples like Great Witley in Worcestershire). There comes a time away from home when one longs for the sight of an English church poking its medieval tower or spire above the trees, or standing gaunt on some windswept rainy hilltop. Or for the special glories of Blythburgh in Suffolk, or the austerity of Salthouse, overlooking the marshlands of the north of Norfolk, and God knows how many beside that dwell in the church-crawler's memory. These are our special contribution to the culture of Western Europe.

It is almost incredible to think that by the end of the eleventh century Norfolk and Suffolk alone had some twelve hundred parish churches standing. Hundreds of those in Norfolk are now in ruins or have disappeared altogether, but Suffolk still has some five hundred left. Kent must have been almost as rich, if only we knew the exact numbers. The eastern side of England was in general the richest for many centuries, until the industrial Midlands and the North took over.

England is a country of towers and spires; some twelve thousand medieval churches remain, so many that one stops every couple of miles or less to see yet another, and all different even if only in subtle ways. And not just the buildings, but their monuments and fittings also: the monuments of dukes and earls as at Bottesford in Leicestershire, of thousands of local squires, of more thousands of local yeomen, all of whom contributed to the making of the English landscape over the centuries. Of them, too, it might be said, standing at the church door and looking out over the fields and walls and hedges: 'If you seek their monument, look around you.'

It has been reckoned that about 230 churches remain which still show Anglo-Saxon work, the earliest dating from the seventh century as at Escomb (plate 39) in the north-east, or Brixworth in the heart of Northamptonshire. In fact, if East Anglia is anything to go by, and it was admittedly the wealthiest part of England in late Saxon times, there must be thousands of English churches standing on pre-Conquest sites with nothing to show in the way of structural evidence of that period. Most of these early churches were rebuilt in the twelfth century (such as Maxey, plate I) and some were new-built at the same time, as at Heath (plate II) to mark the appearance in the landscape of a new village, colonised from the 'waste'.

Who built this multitude of churches so thick upon the ground? In the west especially the first founders were Celtic missionary-saints from Ireland and Wales. In our troubled days it is as well to remember that it was Ireland and its missionaries that kept the Christian faith alive in western Europe when Rome had been overrun by the Barbarians. Their churches in England and Wales are chiefly associated with 'holy wells'. Then there were the greater monasteries like Peterborough that founded churches such as Brixworth in the depths of the Midlands well before 700 AD and the multitude of private landowners who founded their own churches and endowed them. These churches were usually built as close as possible to the lord of the manor's house; but in eastern England, where the social structure was very different, with fewer lords and more free men, churches were founded by such men in some spot convenient to the neighbourhood. Often, therefore, we have the phenomenon in East Anglia of two or even three churches sharing one churchyard. Each church had a different founder or founders, but one site was enough. Reepham in Norfolk originally had three churches in the same yard (now two) and South Walsham in Norfolk also has two adjacent churches. Swaffham Prior (plate 40) is another nice example.

Many churches are now known to have been built on Romano-British sites, and more of these will come to light; and some are clearly built on pagan sites, such as Brentor in Devon, Knowlton in Dorset, or Ellough near Beccles in Suffolk. Harrow is another such case, for the name means 'heathen temple'. Old sites with religious associations were taken over as a deliberate policy.

All over England there came another Great Rebuilding comparable with that of the twelfth century. Older churches were swept away in the century or so between 1420 and 1540, so that much of the English landscape is dotted with Perpendicular churches, some grand like those of the Cotswolds and Suffolk (plate 41) based on new industrial wealth, many poor as in Cornwall, but the best that an ordinary farming community could manage. In these churches the only evidence of an older building is often the Norman font, for the right to baptise was evidence of full parochial status and in the absence of any documentary proof this was the tangible evidence.

With the Reformation, church-building practically ceased for some two hundred years. The exceptions like Staunton Harold in Leicestershire are rare and usually striking for this reason. Instead one sometimes finds remarkable little seventeenth-century nonconformist chapels, a few of which survive almost unchanged, and many more of the placid eighteenth century. Often they stand well away from the village and the medieval church.

Then comes the period of Victorian 'restoration'. Thousands of medieval churches had been allowed to fall into decay, some irreparably. This is the only excuse one can make for the ignorant savagery with which the new rich of the Victorian Age ripped out the old and put in the hard and new. Yet there are fine and original Victorian churches dotted around the English landscape: no church is totally worth unvisiting. Most remarkable of all in modern times is the church of St Mary at Wellingborough, close to the railway and buried among little redbrick streets. It is the masterpiece of Sir Ninian Comper, begun in 1908 and completed externally in 1930. The exterior is not specially inviting, but the interior, richly coloured and flamboyant, is to my mind one of the wonders of England, still, alas, unfinished. It is literally an eye-opener. It gives one a faint idea of the colour and richness of a medieval church and how it must have struck our pioneer forefathers, fresh from their primitive farmsteads and their hard-won fields.

39   Escomb (Durham) is one of a small group of early Anglo-Saxon churches that survive amid sordid surroundings, the others in this district being Monkwearmouth and Jarrow. All date from the late seventh – early eighth centuries, from the time of Bede. Escomb is remarkably completely preserved, a perfect example of its time. This little group are among the earliest remains of Christianity north of the Alps, and probably owe their survival to their squalid industrial surroundings. No rich Victorian squire would have lived here, or he would have had this wonderful monument down in no time.

40   Swaffham Prior (Cambs) is one of the best surviving examples of two churches in one churchyard. The village was formerly divided between two parishes, but they shared a single burial ground. Both churches contain twelfth-century work, but they were probably founded long before this. St Mary (right) is still in use, but the church of St Cyriac and St Julitta – an unusual and ancient dedication also found in Devon – is now abandoned. The tower is c. 1500, but the body of the church is mostly 1806–12. Swaffham Prior itself was probably a Romano-British settlement in origin.

41   Stoke-by-Nayland is one of the grandest of medieval Suffolk churches, much loved by Constable. The superb tower, rising above the Stour valley, is a landmark for miles, built with the money of rich cloth merchants c. 1440–60. This was the richest industrial area of late medieval England. But the glory of this church owed something also to the resident landowners, first the Tendrings and then the Howards (Dukes of Norfolk) who had a great house here. Both families are commemorated by notable brass effigies.

42   Gipping, also in Suffolk, has a different origin from the great cloth and wool churches. It was built as a private chantry-chapel by Sir James Tyrell in 1484–1485 and never achieved full parochial status. It is not only a perfect example of Perpendicular architecture, but a masterpiece of flushwork masonry in flint: almost incredible to think that flints from the local soil could produce such a brilliant result in building.

43   Somerset is rightly famous for its church-towers, mostly late medieval in date. Many of them rise up from 'islands' amid the miles of reclaimed marshland – the Levels. They are superb memorials to the rich abbeys like Glastonbury, which have themselves perished, who reclaimed all this lovely countryside and rebuilt 'their' churches out of surplus revenues. Weston Zoyland, shown here, was largely rebuilt by Richard Bere, abbot of Glastonbury from 1493–1524.

44   Heptonstall stands on a windy hill-top a few miles west of Halifax. It got its first church, as a dependent chapelry of the enormous parish of Halifax, in the twelfth century. There are now two churches in the same churchyard, but not for the same reason as in East Anglia (plate 40). One, the medieval, is now a picturesque ruin, the victim of the Pennine gales, particularly the storm of 1847. The present church was built in 1850–4: Pevsner calls it 'a large and prosperous-looking edifice', but it is more than just that. It is a splendid example of mid-Victorian church-building.

One of the myths about the English landscape, which I hope has been destroyed in the preceding chapters, is that it was mainly the creation of the great landlords in their country houses and their spreading parks, and the ownership and management of their farmlands, and perhaps even the removal of whole villages in order to obtain greater seclusion. To a limited extent this is true – a very limited extent. For an exile from England, until recent years at any rate, would conjure up such a vision of a Georgian country house for preference, with acres of green parkland as a setting, studded with oaks and other fine hardwood trees

> The rich man in his castle,
> The poor man at his gate . . .

The country house, of course, during the four hundred years of its dominance, has had a profound effect on the landscape, much more so in some favoured parts of England than others. Landed magnates might own tens of thousands of acres in the Fenland or in the Lake District, but they did not choose to live there. Many, especially if they were great officers of state, chose to live within a reasonable distance of London. So we find, as a general rule with notable exceptions, that Northamptonshire was as far north as they cared to build their provincial palaces and Wiltshire as far west. Beyond Burghley (plate 46) the great houses are thinner on the ground going northwards; beyond Longleat they thin out to the west. The country houses of Somerset are beautiful (like Montacute) but smaller, and those of Devon smaller still. Great houses and noble families could, indeed, flourish elsewhere but the biggest impact of the country house was within a radius of less than a hundred miles of London.

The first true country houses began to be built round about 1500. It is difficult to define exactly what a 'country house' is, for medieval abbots had their rural retreats; but broadly speaking it is a house built for show and comfort, with no thought of defence: no moats, no gun-ports, no battlements except as a picturesque hangover from the past. The change was not too sudden: even the perfect Compton Wynyates in Warwickshire (plate 45), completed by about 1520, started off with a moat; but possibly this was largely useful for fish and ornamental as reflecting the soft redbrick walls. And the plans of these early country houses, down to the mid-century, were still basically medieval. The 'new fashion' came flooding into England in Elizabeth's reign. At Burghley, William Cecil began building in the mid-fifties of the sixteenth century in the old style, but he finished up with a grand Renaissance palace thirty years later.

The dissolution of the monasteries in the 1530s put an end to one powerful influence in the English landscape and left them in ruins. The country houses took their place, at times almost literally. Not only did the rich and powerful ones acquire the monastic lands from an improvident and vainglorious Henry VIII, but they often bought the materials – the stone, the lead, and the timber –

of the monastic sites and re-used them for a great house on the site or near by. Very few attempted to convert a monastery directly into a house.

Country houses proliferated therefore from the 1540s onwards, built mostly out of the plunder of the monasteries and less often from the profits of legitimate mercantile trade in the city of London.

There were other visual changes. In medieval times, the poor man lived literally at the castle gate; but the new country houses required a park to set them off, and also to separate them physically from the common people: a process completed by the public schools of the nineteenth century. At first these were deer-parks in the medieval tradition. Later these simple parks were 'landscaped' by a few eminent improvers in the eighteenth century. So the old deer park at Burghley, dating from the 1560s, was completely altered by Capability Brown in the mid-eighteenth century, who, as at Blenheim and other grand houses, provided a winding lake to complete the artificial picture, and moved clumps of grown trees to get the maximum visual effect.

Yet the park of the small Georgian squire, with his three or four thousand acres of farmland, rather than the twenty or thirty thousand of the nobleman, is much more characteristic of the English countryside, the modest house half-hidden behind the trees but still not too cut off from the ancestral village.

The greater country houses produced other effects. In not a few places they removed whole villages which stood in the way of a larger park or a better vista and rebuilt them elsewhere, as at Milton Abbas or Stowe or Nuneham Courtenay or Castle Howard. Then, in the nineteenth century, the more benevolent landlords built 'estate villages' such as Wimpole in Cambridgeshire (plate 52), easily recognisable by their Victorian Gothic touches and their similarity of style, unlike a village that has grown haphazardly over several centuries. Even a dull industrial village in the Midlands might still have houses dating from five different centuries.

At the same time as the country houses were going up, there was a flowering of rural England as a whole, right down to the farmhouse and the cottage. I have called this The Age of Prosperity and it is roughly true for my purpose. The rich were growing richer, and the poor poorer, so it was not prosperity for everybody. But it is the surplus wealth that changes a landscape and 'improves' it from time to time. The poor merely work on it and keep it tidy:

> Only a man harrowing clods
>   In a slow silent walk
> With an old horse that stumbles and nods
>   Half asleep as they stalk.

The rich grew richer on the systematic plunder that the Tudor period offered, plunder from lands and offices, from tax evasion, and less often from legitimate trade. But they were not the only gainers: in the provincial towns there were wealthy merchants, rebuilding their old houses in a new style, and in the countryside the larger yeomen were also doing well. It was an age of inflation, fast by Tudor standards, and big farmers were making fortunes. So we get the Great Rebuilding largely in the decades from about 1570 to 1640; then a break during the turmoil of the Civil War and its aftermath, and then the prosperous Georgian age. In the villages the yeomen either modernised their ancestral houses and changed them completely externally (it takes an expert eye nowadays to detect the medieval core of what looks like a thorough going Tudor or Jacobean farmhouse) or else rebuilt them completely (plates 48 and 49). In villages like Chiddingstone (plate 49) a whole street might be recreated, and survive miraculously into the insensitive butchery of our own sad, money-grabbing times.

The richer farmers, combining with their landlords in many places, also transformed their local countrysides. The age of parliamentary enclosure (chapter 7) completely transformed millions of acres from a medieval landscape of hedgeless open fields into a modern pattern of small hedged or walled fields; but a great deal of this fundamental change was going on all through the sixteenth and seventeenth centuries in the interests of better farming. It was enclosure by private agreement, not by parliamentary act, but it produced the same visual effect except that often these earlier enclosed fields were larger than the later. Visually one can often detect them on the ground by the greater size of the fields (generally pastures) and more obviously by the number of gated and unhedged roads, winding airily through the seventeenth-century landscape. The gates are rapidly disappearing before the impatient fury of motorists: walkers did not mind the slight break and the chance to pause and lean over a view: but the roads remain largely unhedged to this day. This sort of visual change in the landscape went on unsystematically, depending on the number of farmers involved and the relationship between them and the squire, whose consent was essential to such changes. So even in the rural Midlands one can walk from one parish into the next and pass from the mid-sixteenth century into the early nineteenth, and back again into the seventeenth. One immediate clue to such changes in time is the size and complexity of the hedgerows (see chapter 3).

There were other changes in the landscape in this long age of surplus wealth. In the villages one finds so many attractive almshouses and grammar schools dating from the late sixteenth century to the middle of the seventeenth. In medieval times such surplus wealth as there was – and even poor widows could give a penny now and then – went to the repair or rebuilding of the parish church (plate 41) and to glorifying it with painted windows, rood screens, and new benches. But after the Reformation this practical form of piety ceased. Churches were barely kept in repair, and almost none was built for a hundred years or more after 1540. It was a more secular age, and the surplus wealth of merchant, clothier, and yeoman, and country gentleman was bequeathed to the founding of a row of almshouses as at Weekley near Kettering (1611) and hundreds of other villages and small towns, or to a new school as at Ashbourne in Derbyshire in 1586 (plate 50). The village of Weekley also got a Free School in 1624. A remarkable amount of the money for these almshouses and schools came from successful merchants in the city of London, who had been born in the provinces and made their fortunes in the capital; but they did not forget their country origins. Many a famous and not-so-famous grammar school in England owes its foundation to such men: the overweening wealth of London returned to fertilise rural England abundantly. Many of the original schools have been lost to us, especially those in the large towns where the supply of scholars outgrew them, but in some of the smaller towns such as Ashbourne the old building stands. In little Rutland the original school buildings of 1584 still survive intact at Uppingham and Oakham and are still used as classrooms.

The building of country houses did not cease with the Georgian period. For the big landlords — though individual families might well have their vicissitudes — estates grew vaster and vaster. To him that hath shall be given, from him that hath not shall be taken away even that which he hath. Such a grand house as Panshanger in Hertfordshire is essentially of the nineteenth century, with marvellous landscaping by Humphrey Repton and his son. Many English country houses are no older than this. Perhaps the last country house to be built in this country is Castle Drogo, built by Lutyens between 1910 and 1930, 'an extravaganza in granite' on the edge of Dartmoor of all places, but built with money from trade in London. Gordon Selfridge's notion of building a monstrous house on the Dorset coast mercifully never came off. In our own time, scores of country houses are left to decay every year or are demolished outright. Their great age is over. After the war of 1914–18 it became too difficult to keep such grandeur going, and so many heirs to great estates had also perished in the fighting 'leading their men'.

The last impact of the country house on the landscape, on any sort of scale, was the restoration of the neglected churches on their large estates. A landed magnate might have the patronage of a dozen or a score of village churches, and a rich and conscientious landlord might well lavish his surplus wealth, or some of it, on 'restoring' the churches for which he felt responsible. Too often the results were lamentable: there was too much money. Much needed doing after centuries of neglect, but much could also have been saved and lovingly restored if money had been a bit shorter. Many ancient churches were completely rebuilt in a hard and unsympathetic way. The Rolles in Devon, the largest and richest landowners, uglified pretty well every church they touched with their great wealth. No doubt this is an ungracious remark, and many a Victorian church has by now acquired an atmosphere of its own, and many more will do so; so perhaps the prosperous Victorian squire and magnate will be blessed in another century.

The Age of Prosperity, however long it lasted, and however few it permanently touched, had a profound effect on the English countryside. One sees its marks everywhere. Try as we will, we cannot erase them altogether, even as we cannot erase in the last resort the landscapes of medieval times, of the Old English and the Roman, and even the prehistoric.

45   Compton Wynyates was one of the earliest true country-houses to be built. It was built by Sir William Compton and probably finished by 1520. It has been called 'the most perfect picture-book house of the Early Tudor decades' set in a lovely small park. There was once a village here – deserted long ago – hence the parish church some little way off. Built of brick, the house glows in the afternoon sun like a rich old burgundy. It originally had a moat (which was drained in the Civil War) and to this extent had not entirely abandoned the medieval idea of defence.

46   Burghley House, though begun in the 1550s by Sir William Cecil, is essentially a magnificent Elizabethan palace largely carried through in the decade 1577–1587. Like Castle Ashby, in the same county, it stands 'four-square and self-confident as only Elizabethan and Jacobean houses can be' (Pevsner). Houses of this splendour were built mostly by the great officers of state at this period. The park, once a natural deer-park, was landscaped by Capability Brown in the mid-eighteenth century; and when he had finished he had created one of the most perfect 'artificial' landscapes in England.

47   Walden Place at Saffron Walden is a perfect mid-Georgian red-brick house, totally representative of its period and social class: the 'grounds' rather than the grand park: built for prosperous eighteenth-century gentry. Something utterly English.

48   Leys Farm, just outside Weobley in Herefordshire, is dated 1589. Completely characteristic of the richly-timbered yeoman's house of the Elizabethan period, of the Great Rebuilding. Yet touches of the medieval remain with the porch at the lower end of a central hall and not placed symmetrically. The Welsh Border country is specially rich in this kind of timber-building. Weobley village is spectacularly so, and so is Pembridge not far away. This part of England was still rich in woodland timber when the East Midlands had been seriously denuded.

49   Sometimes the 'Great Rebuilding' produced whole streets of sixteenth- and seventeenth-century building, like this one at Chiddingstone in Kent – almost too perfect. The houses are timber framed, sometimes tile-hung, sometimes filled with brick-nogging: all homely materials out of the local soil. These are all good Yeoman-houses in a prosperous age in a naturally rich county. No wonder at the saying that 'When hospitality dies in England, she will give her last groan among the Yeomen of Kent.'

50   All over England, in large towns and small, and even in villages, grammar schools were founded by local benefactors. This is Ashbourne Grammar School in Derbyshire, founded in 1586 by 'divers well-disposed citizens of London, desirous . . . not to be named, being born in or near to Ashbourne in the Peak . . . combining their loving benevolence together.' A London fish-monger, no doubt a native of Ashbourne also, founded an almshouse here in 1608. So the wealth of London flowed freely into the provinces, creating new townscapes in the most remote places.

51   For the greater landlords, the Age of Prosperity lasted right down to 1914. The Hon. Newton Fellows built Eggesford house in 1830 in a romantic medieval style, on a commanding site in mid-Devon. Thomas Hardy was once a guest here. It is now a very picturesque ruin.

52   Wimpole in Cambridgeshire, seat of the Earls of Hardwicke, is the greatest mansion in the county. But besides the great house, the Hardwickes, with their 20,000 acres or so of land, rebuilt the village c. 1845 as an 'estate village'. This was a fairly common period for such benevolent gestures. Most counties can show a good example or two. A late example (early twentieth century) is Horninghold in Leicestershire.

Until well on in time the greater part of the English landscape was unplanned, above all in the Highland Zone of the west and north of the country. Here the fields, the winding lanes, the hedgebanks and the wriggling walls, were the work of millions of now-unknown peasants and their families, working with the only tools they possessed – the axe, the mattock, and the spade. Hence the smallness of fields created in this way, and their irregular shape as they met obstacles and moved around them rather than waste time moving a huge tree or a massive boulder. It was a landscape made piecemeal, almost yard by yard. In a sense one could say that the open fields of the Lowland Zone were planned, as new land was brought in from the surrounding waste and allocated into strips and furlongs, but again it was piecemeal and on a small scale. The complexity of this medieval and earlier landscape can still be glimpsed in the intricate pattern of ridge-and-furrow (plate 53) where the old-time arable had been converted to pasture and the plough ceased to disturb the soil. The ancient pattern was fossilised under grass, and much of it remained so until the recent war. Since then larger machinery has helped to spread the destruction of the pattern, which ought to have been mapped in detail while there was time. Now it is difficult to do this except in patches.

The disappearance of the open-field landscape began early in some parts of England. In Devon, for example, it was being enclosed with hedges from the thirteenth century onwards, probably because it was realised even then that the terrain and climate were better suited to pastoral farming, and smaller fields with hedges meant better control of the stock. Much more enclosure with hedges and ditches took place in the fifteenth and sixteenth centuries (see chapter 4), creating large-scale pastures almost like ranches to begin with; though later these were broken up into smaller fields for better control and greater shelter. In a sense, too, this was planning, but to a very limited degree. It cannot be compared with the professional planning that came in with the parliamentary enclosure movement in Georgian and later times.

The social impact of this widespread erasure of the open field landscapes was, and still is, hotly contested by contemporaries and historians. This is not my concern here; what is more to the point is that there were, even at the time, wide divergences of view about the visual effect upon the old landscape. Thus the Rev. James Tyley, in Clare's heartland, attacked the open fields as 'unbroken tracts that strained and tortured the sight'. But a Leicestershire historian (Throsby) said in 1790 of a scene in the Welland valley:

> In passing from this place [Medbourne] towards Welham, I saw a sight as gratifying to my senses; a fine, open field, the blades of corn about four inches high, and as free from weeds and filth as the best-managed garden in the kingdom. People who live surrounded by enclosures, or at a distance from open fields, would, at the sight of this, be in raptures. The land, I believe, is good, and tillage seems carried to its highest perfection. To ditch and quick it [i.e. plant hawthorn hedges] for inclosure, with offensive intersect-

ing lines, would detroy the finest monument of what this country has been, with respect to openfield tillage, that remains among us.

Part of this difference of aesthetic opinion about open-field landscape may well have arisen from a difference in topography. In Clare's country, bordering the Fens, the open fields may have seemed dreary and monotonous because of their very flatness; but where the landscape undulated, was dotted with little groves of full-grown trees for shade, the visual effect was quite otherwise, as those who know the open field landscapes of southern Bavaria will agree, especially about the time of harvest when thousands of acres of waving corn ripple away to a far horizon.

There was the same conflict of opinion about the heaths and commons that survived, though here poets like John Clare were heavily outnumbered by the 'improvers'. In Suffolk, for example, George Crabbe wrote savage lines about the village heath and the kind of feckless ne'er-do-wells who got a meagre living off the heath and the neighbouring sea:

> Here joyless roam a wild amphibious race,
> With sullen woe display'd in every face;
> Who far from civil arts and social fly,
> And scowl at strangers with suspicious eye.

Yet today the heathlands of Suffolk, bordering the coast and running inland towards delectable little towns or coloured woods, are a magical landscape at any time of the year, criss-crossed with sandy tracks that have not changed from time immemorial. Clare's poetry about his native heath at Helpston is too well known to quote – and yet I must:

> Ye commons left free in the rude rags of nature,
> Ye brown heaths beclothed in furze as ye be,
> My wild eye in rapture adores every feature,
> Ye are as dear as this heart in my bosom to me.

Every invasion of his native heath (and how well-founded this old form of words is!) was like a knife-wound to the heart. One can still feel as Clare did when the 'developers' move into one's native town and mow down without knowledge or sentiment the buildings and streets and lanes of one's childhood, with their bulging money-grubbing eyes. For they are busy destroying even with their greedy eyes, before their machines move in for the kill. Clare saw the surveyors for the coming railway walking over his heath, notebook in hand. How well one knows that symbol of coming destruction and longs to seize and burn it! The replanning of the English landscape affected nearly $2\frac{1}{2}$ million acres of open fields, most of it accomplished between 1750 and 1850. On top of this more than two million acres of commons and 'wastes' were enclosed; but the visual effect on the commons and heaths was much less. On the open-field arable it was a total revolution in the landscape. Millions of acres, mostly in a broad belt running from Northumberland down to Dorset, were replanned by a rural professional class: surveyors, lawyers, and local gentry. Accurate maps were drawn of the old open fields, and every detail of their strips, furlongs, headlands, trackways, and other evidences of a thousand-year-old culture; claims were heard (on the whole fairly: the fault lay in the expensive machinery which the peasant could not afford or understand); and then the straight lines were drawn on the old maps to mark the boundaries of new fields and the new roads. A whole parish, a complete and ancient landscape, could be transformed in a couple of years.

It is a pattern of straight lines everywhere – dead-straight hedgerows of hawthorn interspersed with the occasional ash to break the monotony – for it is a monotonous landscape over most of the Midlands, relieved only by the fact that the older enclosures intervene, parishes enclosed back in Elizabethan and Stuart times, where the pattern and the feeling are immediately different. One passes a particular hedgerow, unless warned beforehand by the one-inch map showing the parish boundaries, and moves from a dull uniformity laid down in the late 1700s or the early 1800s, into a more spacious landscape left over from four hundred years ago – thicker hedgerows with a greater variety of shrubs and weeds, and often larger and airier fields.

The enclosure award issued by the local committee, to give the Enclosure Commissioners a more prosaic name, laid out a new field pattern all over the parish, except for the 'ancient enclosures' that lay behind the village homesteads – the 'toft and croft' of medieval village records. Once his land was allotted, an owner had to make a hedge around the perimeter of his allotment within twelve months or suffer a severe penalty. This was for the very practical reason that the annual harvest could not wait for bureaucrats to arrive at finicky decisions or for some lazy farmer to hold up the entire planning operation. After making his perimeter hedge, of quickset (hawthorn) in some parts or stone walls in others (plates 29, 30), the owner or occupier could then be left to divide his new farm into smaller units by internal hedges. For pasture-farming a field of ten acres was reckoned to be best for good stock control: another element in the monotony of many a Midland landscape (plate 53). Now the modern farmer, where the old Midland pastures are being re-converted to arable, is busy ripping out these internal hedges and restoring the older landscape.

In the Midlands the ash was the favourite tree for planting in the new hedges, with young hawthorn to form an impenetrable fence. In Suffolk, holly and oak were often used. In the north of England the noble sycamore was used for this purpose, largely as a windbreak for farmhouses and fields against that fierce climate. In the Midlands, especially, the home of lordly fox-hunting even before the parliamentary enclosures, the landscape was embellished with artificial fox-covers, pretty regular in shape, unlike an old woodland, and these bear the names of the time, such as Lord Morton's Covert in east Leicestershire or Botany Bay not far away.

The enclosure commissioners also replanned the roads of the parish, usually in straight lines. There seems to have been a standard width of forty feet for inter-village roads, sixty-six feet for roads to a market-town, and up to ninety-nine feet for a main road to London. These are extraordinary widths even by modern standards but they were intended to carry traffic all through a muddy winter before the days of hard road surfaces such as McAdam introduced in the early nineteenth century. Not all communities responded to the cost of macadamising their roads with joyous speed – some delayed well into the century – but then a twelve-foot width or so was enough, so that the straight enclosure roads now have a more or less narrow hard ribbon down the middle (occasionally well to one side) and we are left with the wide grass verges that are such a striking feature of the landscape of the Midlands and eastern England: once the wild home of cow-parsley and the dog-rose and other lovely English weeds and flowers, now under constant attack by the weed-killers and the cutting-machinery of insensitive County Councils.

Clare saw his little world transformed well within his lifetime. John Steane makes this point imaginatively, for the new landscape of Helpston in Clare's countryside was radically changed in more ways than one. It was not just the heath that changed. 'Clare's vision', says Steane, 'was limited by the village which was the centre of a road system designed as an internal network to connect different places within the parish. This microcosmic universe was shattered by the work of the rural professional class and the new topography of enclosure was imposed on Clare's world. The ancient internal lanes vanished. Helpston was connected to the outside world with straight roads. The parish now simply became a place on the way to somewhere else. The linear landscape replaced a circular one . . .' One look at the Ordnance Survey map for the Helpston countryside and what lies around it reveals how true this observation is.

One last change remains to be discussed. With the complete reorganisation of the open fields, many farmers found that their lands lay well out in the parish if not near the frontier. Under the old system, it is true, their hundreds of strips had been scattered all over the parish, but the village was still the centre in which it was most convenient to live for farming purposes. Under the new system there was no need to live in the village unless you were fortunate enough to have your new lands not far away. So the richer farmers at least built themselves new houses in the middle of their lands within a short time of the enclosure. Quebec Farm (colour plate VII) gives itself away by its name. In fact the parish of Sileby in which it lies was enclosed in 1760 and Quebec Farm commemorates Wolfe's victory in Canada.

Many of the smaller farmers could not afford to build a new house in the fields and stayed on in the ancestral village. It was all a matter of money. In times of prosperity more farmers could break away, as at Glatton in Huntingdonshire, but in neighbouring Great Gidding, enclosed much later in a time of farming depression, nobody could face the cost of a new house (plate 57): so here we have a complete contrast in two parishes lying next to each other. Every place has its own secret history, and much of it is reflected in the local landscape. In Dorset geology lay behind this change, or rather lack of it. Nobody built a new house out in the fields after enclosure in these parts for the simple reason that, in the chalklands at least, there was no water-supply. Instead, the landscape is dotted with groups of barns and sheds arranged around yards which acted as the centre of farming activity: but the farmhouse stayed in the village.

53   The medieval pattern of strips and furlongs in the open fields was by no means completely obliterated at the parliamentary enclosure of the fields. This remarkable pattern of ridge-and-furrow comes from the heart of Northamptonshire, where it is widespread and was far more common before the ploughing-up campaign during the recent war. The pre-enclosure pattern has been preserved solely because over much of the east Midlands the land was turned over to pastures long ago, and the strips fossilised under grass.

54   Few places in England retain their open-field landscape but occasionally it survives by some accident. This pattern is at Forrabury near the north coast of Cornwall. Though most of the original strips have been amalgamated to form larger units, the strips on the left, especially the curving ones, retain their identity. Braunton in north Devon also retains a large piece of open-field landscape but it is diminishing every year.

55 The parliamentary enclosure of the old open fields imposed a regular pattern
    upon the older landscape: small fields with straight hedgerows, planted with
    hawthorn and at intervals with ash. The farmstead out in the fields is also
    characteristic, built after the medieval landscape had been completely re-
    planned. Near by is Moscow Farm which gives some idea of the date of this
    particular landscape near Burrough-on-the-Hill in Leicestershire.   83

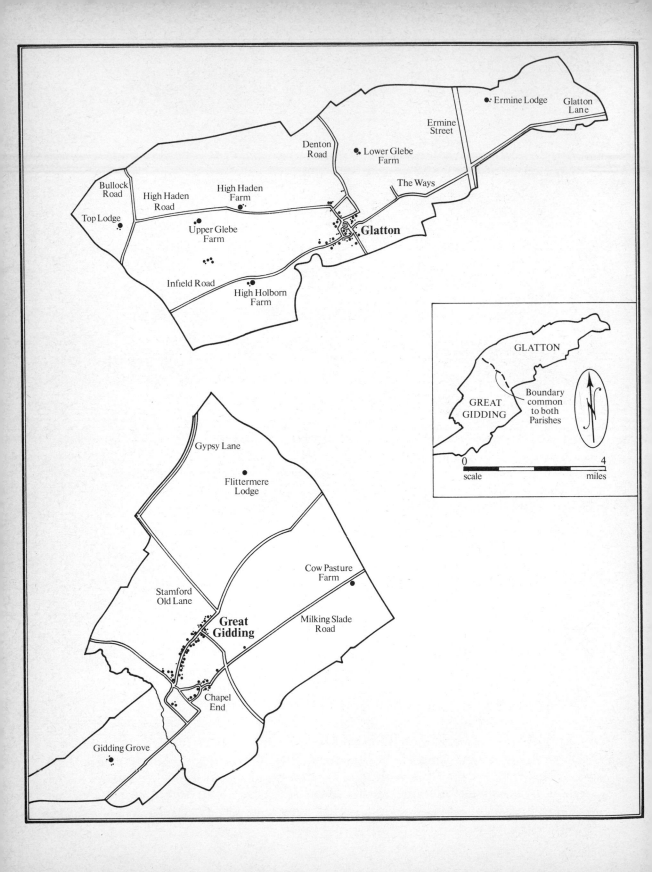

Bullock Road

Top Lodge

High Haden Road

Upper Glebe Farm

High Haden Farm

Infield Road

High Holborn Farm

Denton Road

Lower Glebe Farm

The Ways

Ermine Street

Ermine Lodge

Glatton Lane

Glatton

Gypsy Lane

Flittermere Lodge

Cow Pasture Farm

Stamford Old Lane

Great Gidding

Milking Slade Road

Chapel End

Gidding Grove

GLATTON

GREAT GIDDING

Boundary common to both Parishes

0   scale   4   miles

56 & 57   Generally, but not always, the parliamentary enclosure and replanning of the field-pattern in a particular parish led to the building of new farmhouses out in the new fields for convenience of farming. Not all farmers could afford to build new houses. At Glatton (top) we get this landscape of new farmhouses built after the enclosure, and the ancestral village diminished. But at Great Gidding, the adjacent parish (below), the enclosure came late in the nineteenth century, at a time of the farming depression. Nobody could afford to build, so the farmhouses stayed in the village and the fields remained empty.

58 & 59   This roadside view in Rutland (top) is very characteristic of a landscape enclosed by the planners: straight roads, wide grass verges rich in weeds and wild flowers, the hawthorns in full bloom. Here the usual hawthorn hedge has been replaced by one of local limestone. The naturalist W. H. Hudson always regarded the 18th of May as the crown of the Midland year, when normally the flowering hawthorns were at their peak and scented the entire countryside. Below is a very wide 'enclosure road' because it is running between a village and its market-town, and the planners allowed for this additional traffic.

60   The commons and 'wastes' were generally enclosed decades later than the open-field arable fields lower down. This scene on the high moorland of Ewe Moor near Malham in west Yorkshire, enclosed as late as 1845, shows the kind of dry walling that divided the old commons between those farms in the dale which had ancient common rights. Sheep no longer wandered at large over thousands of acres but were confined within these bounds, though even so the enclosures were very large.

The late G. K. Chesterton said many silly things, the worst of which was his stupid judgement on Thomas Hardy, a man who stood head and shoulders above him in English literature. He uttered a milder silliness when he wrote

> Before the Roman came to Rye or out to Severn strode,
> The rolling English drunkard made the rolling English road.

These inspired lines seem to have stuck in the popular memory, though they were, and are, complete nonsense. Before the straightening out of many of the old roads in the turnpike age of the seventeenth and eighteenth centuries, and the even greater straightening-out of modern times in the interests of higher speeds for lethal machines, most English roads – even main roads – meandered from place to place. I am not thinking especially of the lanes of south-western England, handmade a thousand years ago, still wandering from hamlet to farm, and from farm to farm, too great a mileage for even the fiercest county surveyor to dream about; or of the lanes of Suffolk, which make a pattern like loose knitting on the map; or of the local lanes and tracks that Wordsworth wrote about in his *Guide through the District of the Lakes*. Any look at a good late eighteenth-century map on a large scale will show that even the main roads rarely take a straight course between towns.

The prehistoric trackways of the chalk and limestone uplands naturally take a more direct course. They had unlimited space on both sides, and were often very broad and not too well defined.

But why, for example, should the A149 along the north coast of Norfolk from Hunstanton to Cromer wander as it does through comparatively flat country, curving frequently along the margin of the marshland to the north and the arable and heath on the south, curves that make the road so delightful to travel along at moderate speed, wondering what fresh vista lies around the next curve or corner? In this case I think we must seek its wandering course ultimately in the trackway first made perhaps by prehistoric cattle as they drifted along, feeding from side to side as they went, trampling a path through the woods and the heaths before turning into the marshes in the summer months. It was cattle that first trampled out the lines of many of our main roads some two thousand or more years ago. Their drivers naturally followed the same wiggling path.

But the main road did not come into existence direct from these cattle-paths: apart from the Romans no national system of main roads was ever thought out in this country. When villages were founded, these beaten paths and tracks, or some of them, were naturally taken over as the ready-made route between one village and the next. The road network in Anglo-Saxon times was simply an inter-village system, if one could call it that; and below that an inter-farm system where the isolated farm and not the village was the most common form of human habitation. It is said that Devon, where the isolated farmstead and hamlet predominate, has a greater mileage of roads (that is, roads looked after by an authority and not including mere rough tracks to really isolated farms) than the whole of Belgium.

Out of this inchoate pattern of inter-village paths there developed a thin network of main roads from one important trading centre to another. Some of these may go back to pre-Conquest times, but in the main they were developed in the twelfth and thirteenth centuries when a great number of new towns appeared in the landscape or when old towns grew rapidly in local and national importance. Then we find the inter-village paths being used as links in a line between two important towns, and where there was a gap in the old network a new piece was inserted to fill the hole. By the early fourteenth century, the well-known Gough map shows a network – albeit not densely made – over the whole of England of roads that set out from London to all parts of the kingdom, roads like the Great North Road to the Scottish border or the Great West Road that eventually finished, as it does today, at Land's End. Even so, it took some time to finalise the line of even a national road (plate 62): there could be all sorts of local diversions and re-routings when great landlords like monasteries planted a big complex of buildings where they thought fit. Centuries later, the owners of great country houses similarly diverted roads in order to tidy up or to extend their parks, and one still makes a sweeping curve around a high park wall put up a hundred or two hundred years ago.

The Romans in general built a system of straight roads (wherever possible: in some upland country even they could not tackle severe gradients head-on) and often of stone setts (plate 61). Many of their roads, however, were made of rammed gravel and survive often as mere hedge-lines and perhaps a faintly marked *agger* across a few fields. And we still have to recover possibly thousands of miles of local Romano-British roads, linking villas to the nearest town, as Margary did so brilliantly in the Weald of Kent and Sussex. Roman roads continued in use well into medieval times: many are used to this day.

The 'drove roads' of England, too, remain largely unexplored. These were the wide grassy tracks by which cattle and sheep were driven from old pastures to new fattening pastures, and later to the great markets of the Midlands and eventually London. Some of the best-marked of these drove roads are those that cross the Cheviots from Scotland into England. There was similarly a number of well-recognised routes over the Border from Wales into England, from at least the thirteenth century onwards. One of these is still called the Welsh Road on the large-scale maps and can be traced from the Welsh Border down into Buckinghamshire: it needs detective work beyond that point. Another drove road crossed the Midlands from north-east to south-west, apparently beginning in the fat pastures of the Welland valley and ending at the famous cattle-market of Banbury. This so-called Banbury Lane crossed the Welsh Road in the mid-Northamptonshire village of Culworth, unknown to fame today, but once a great junction and a market on its own. Some of the quietest English villages have had their generations of glory.

Medieval roads were not as bad as the books make out, or why should we have such superb bridges built in the fifteenth century or the early sixteenth, like that at St Ives (plate 63) and the series of fine bridges over the

Tamar between Devon and Cornwall? Such superb bridges were not built to lead on to muddy tracks. Then comes the turnpike era: old roads were improved and straightened in places, so that here and there one comes across a narrow grass-grown track leaving the present road and tackling a steep hill or plunging down into a deep valley. These are the bits that the turnpike engineers cut off, and they give us a good idea of what a medieval road looked like except that they are high in vegetation, being unused today except by those who seek rare birds and other shy life.

As for the motorways, the less said about them the better. They have at their best a magnificence of line and design; but they are not for the explorer of the minutiae of the English landscape. They are boring in the extreme (plate 65). But at least they have left on one side some pleasant main roads that have now returned to the quietude of a pre-motor car age.

The rivers and canals of England have created their own special landscapes. River traffic was important in medieval England, perhaps even in Roman times to judge by the artificial *lodes* in the Cambridgeshire Fens as at Reach and Burwell (plates 66 and 67). Any place called Hythe is likely to be a decayed medieval river-port and worth going to see. There are usually clear evidences of a flat area, now grass-covered, where the old quay once stood to accommodate river-boats and barges. The Somerset Levels have a number of these ancient river-ports and most of them make excellent picnic places.

After the rivers, with their improved navigations, come the canals. The Romans constructed the Car Dyke, which joined the cornlands of Cambridgeshire to the military garrison at Lincoln. It can still be traced with some difficulty wandering along the Fen Edge; and they also made the Foss Dyke which connected the Trent and the Witham (plate 35). Then an enormous interval until the remarkable achievement of the Exeter Ship Canal (plate 68) in the 1560s, constructed by a city council of merchants far ahead of their time. Brindley and his canals appear on the scene a full two hundred years later, the interval being accounted for by many attempts to improve the existing main rivers like the Severn and the Thames and a score of others.

The Canal Mania, as it was called, produced some beautiful landscapes, chiefly in the Midlands and the North where the new large-scale industry needed cheap transport; they were important visually, too, because in the Midlands above all, large sheets of natural water were uncommon: no coasts, no lakes, only local ponds and streams. And the canals brought their own special kind of buildings: wharves (plate 70), corn-mills as at Shardlow, warehouses, quays for unloading coal in remote country districts, lovely Sheraton-bowed redbrick bridges of hand-made brick, soft and shining in the sun, towpaths, inns, and lock-keepers' cottages. It was a whole new world, which jaded town-dwellers in overcrowded England are beginning to discover for themselves. There were even new towns like Stourport in Worcestershire, a most distinctive kind of town and architecture; and Shardlow in Derbyshire (plate 69) which became a sort of Clapham Junction for the canal traffic of the East Midlands. It is hard to imagine the social revolution, too, that canals brought about in country districts. When the Oxford Canal reached Banbury from Coventry in March 1778 the church-bells pealed all day, brass bands pumped away joyfully, and there was the usual civic dinner. Not least, the price of coal at Banbury wharf came down to one shilling a hundredweight; and on the map of the local countryside there came to be marked numerous small roads called Coal Lane.

The coming of the railways made a harsher immediate impact on the countryside, especially where great engineering works were involved such as the Boxmoor embankment and the Blisworth Cutting (plates 71, 72) leaving bare wounds for miles at a time and also creating earthworks greater than anything seen since the Iron Age hill-forts. No wonder that the aged Wordsworth trumpeted from remote Grasmere

> Is then no nook of English ground secure
> From rash assault?

But Nature clothed the wounds with plant-life in a very short time: indeed new species of plants travelled farther afield and flourished in deep cuttings. Some five thousand miles of railroad had been constructed by the late 1840s. Apart from the late arrival of the Great Central in London (in 1899) the railway network was complete by the 1880s with nearly seventeen thousand miles. Few places in England were far from a railway station, a special kind of architecture which is now being studied and 'collected'.

The canals languished and many closed, but here and there a more profitable one staggered on into the 1920s, like the Nottingham and Grantham Canal, opened in the height of the Canal Mania in 1793 and finally closed in 1929: weed-covered, winding away with scarcely a perceptible movement, except at the decaying locks, through silent fields. Like the abandoned drove-roads, their crumbling towpaths now make some of the safest walking and they cannot be obliterated except in and near the industrial towns.

Now the little country railways decay (plate 74) and all is Inter-City. The railway map of Norfolk looks as barren as it did in the 1850s, and silent cuttings mark where a useful country line wound along from one small market town to the next. Vandals seek out and destroy the wayside stations, though some have been converted into attractive dwelling-houses: weeds and shrubs flourish high where the track is taken up. Miles away one might just hear the dull roar of a fast main-line train taking people from a dismal illiberal life in Birmingham to a dismal illiberal life in London; then peace descends again on the weeds and wild flowers and the birds. Nature takes over quickly wherever Man neglects or abandons his handiwork.

61   The Romans built thousands of miles of roads in Britain, though not all were metalled like this stretch at Blackstone Edge on a road that ran from Littleborough in Lancashire (near Rochdale) towards Ilkley in Yorkshire over the topmost ridge of the Pennines. This is the most remarkable surviving stretch of Roman road in Britain, a pavement of stone setts sixteen feet wide supported by kerbs, with ditches each side for drainage on these rainswept moors. It is in wild places like this, looking at the original road, that one feels deeply the far-reaching power of the Roman Empire.

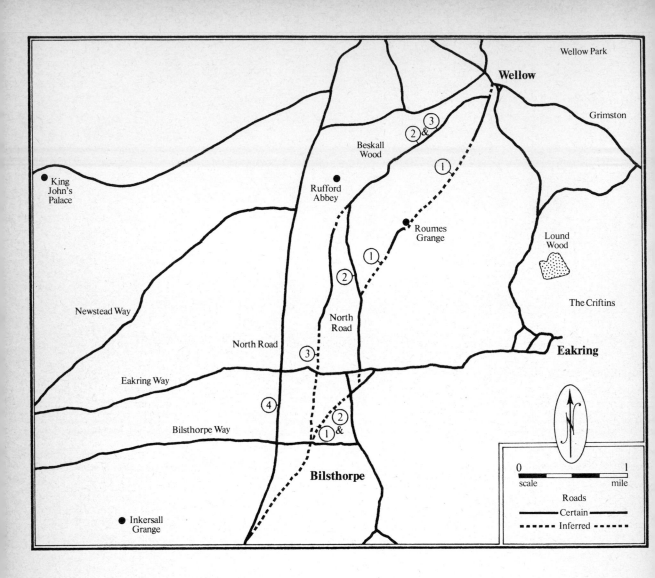

Even before the motorways, the major main roads of England, of which the Great North Road was the best known, looked as if they were the product of some master-planning, even if they were far from straight. But this detailed map of a stretch near Wellow in Nottinghamshire, the history of which has been worked out closely, shows that all sorts of local changes and deviations could take place before the final line was settled and metalled. (1) The earliest line of the North Road prior to 1150. (2) Diversion following the foundation of Rufford Abbey. (3) Line of road on map of 1637. (4) Present line.

63   The fifteenth century saw the building or rebuilding of a great number of important bridges, like this superb one over the Great Ouse at St Ives in Huntingdonshire. It was built about 1415, and retains its original cutwaters and a charming little medieval chapel (1426).

64   Ivybridge, in south Devon, has always been on the main road between Plymouth and Exeter. When Celia Fiennes travelled round England on horseback in the 1690s, she described the road round here as so narrow and deep that an army could march unobserved, and so narrow that even single horses could scarcely pass each other. This road was turnpiked early in the nineteenth century and vastly improved. Here we see the mail-coach of about 1830 stopping at the local inn. Today the road is the murderous A38.

65   The first of the new motorways – the M1 – at the Pepperstock Junction near Luton. This is a ghastly infliction on the English landscape, and worse things have been done since in the West Midlands. Yet there are places where one feared the worst and the results have been good, for example where the M6 goes in lovely sweeping curves through Charnwood Forest in Leicestershire.

66   Reach in Cambridgeshire is a remarkable little place. It was the principal medieval port for Cambridge at least as far back as the twelfth century, though the lode or canal that connected it with the Cam is of Roman construction. The grass-grown Hythe shown here was the actual port with quays and no doubt warehouses. Reach Fair dated from Henry I's time (c. 1120) and was held on the large Green at the top end of the village (see front cover, which also shows the location of the Hythe).

67   The Fenland, with its network of rivers and scores of 'lodes' or artificial channels linking villages to the main system, had many thriving little river-ports. Burwell was one of these. Like Reach (plate 66), Burwell has its Hythe, and various basins and canals. Most of the houses on the west side of the village street were those of local merchants and most of them had their private basins or docks at the back, opening out towards the main lode. Some of these are now grass-grown, but several (about eighteen) are quite recognisable still.

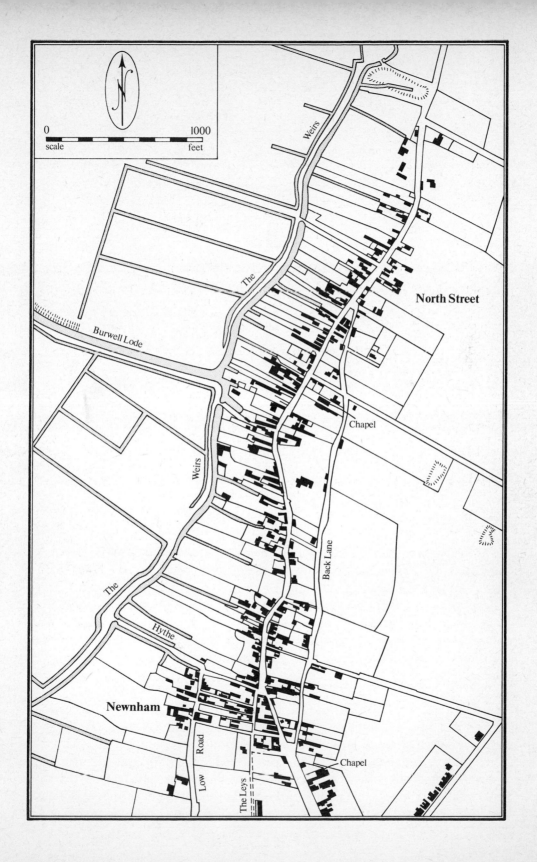

North Street

Weirs

The

Burwell Lode

Chapel

Weirs

Back Lane

The

Hythe

Newnham

Low Road

The Leys

Chapel

0   1000
scale   feet

68 The Exeter ship canal is the oldest canal of its kind in England if one excepts the Roman Foss Dyke which joined the Trent and Witham. The navigable river Exe (right) was blocked for centuries by weirs. After vain attempts to remove these, the city fathers decided to make a canal which would bypass the river. The earliest stretch was in use in 1566. It was twice extended and deepened later. This view shows where the present canal (extended to this point in 1829) rejoins the Exe estuary. It is little used now for trade but clearly has other valuable uses today.

69 & 70 Shardlow (top) was one of the busiest canal ports in England in its time. The Trent and Mersey Canal, one of the key routes of the age, reached here in 1777. The actual junction with the Trent is a mile lower down, but a main road crossed the canal here which made it a good place for transhipment. The Oxford Canal (below) was much slower in completion. Starting from Coventry in 1769, it did not reach Oxford until 1790. Lower Heyford, shown here, had its small wharf, again sited here because a good medieval bridge crossed at this point.

71 & 72   While the railways were under construction they created as much devastation and heart-burning as the motorways of today. Boxmoor embankment on the London and Birmingham Railway looked like this in 1837. Such gigantic works had not been seen since prehistoric times. Below is the Blisworth cutting in October 1838, completed. This cutting has now been doubled in width and revetted with blue brick, so that we have lost its gorge-like appearance.

73   Saltash Bridge (or more correctly the Royal Albert Bridge) under construction by the great Victorian engineer I. K. Brunel. Opened in 1859 it linked Cornwall to the rest of England. This was Brunel's masterpiece and it still carries main-line rail traffic. Brunel scarcely lived to see his great work, but was carried across it on a specially built truck just before he died.

74   The end of the line: the railway from Okehampton reached Lydford (shown here) in 1874, and was extended to Tavistock two years later. It was closed in 1969 after less than a hundred years of life. No doubt the rails have gone by now and the weeds are a yard higher. Already these disused railways have become a part of the English landscape, some of them much more picturesque than this scene of dereliction.

England was the first country to undergo what is commonly called the Industrial Revolution, though historians are not agreed when this revolution really began. But certainly there was considerable industrial activity in this country in Roman times, both in metals and in cloth-working. These earliest activities have left little or no discoverable trace in the modern landscape, having been buried by later generations. Thus the extensive diggings in the Forest of Dean, known as The Scowles, between Lydney and Bream, were first worked by the Romans but most of what we see now is medieval working. There is, however, one mine in Lydney Park, within a small fortified enclosure dating from the first century BC. This enclosure was occupied about three hundred years later by a group of Romano-British miners, who sank a shaft some eighteen feet deep to get at the iron ore. Nothing of this appears, however, on the surface; and the same probably applies to the Romano-British lead-workings at and near Snailbeach in Shropshire.

Perhaps the best of our early industrial landscapes, because it survives to this day in an easily recognisable form, is the countryside around Halifax and above all just west of Heptonstall, towards the high Lancashire border. Defoe, in his classic *Tour through the Whole Island of Great Britain*, made in the 1720s, describes this piece of country pretty well as we see it today. He came over the top from the Lancashire side and approaching Halifax observes:

> the nearer we came to Hallifax, we found the houses thicker, and the villages greater in every bottom; and not only so, but the sides of the hills, which were very steep every way, were spread with houses, and that very thick; for the land being divided into small enclosures, that is to say from two acres to six or seven acres each, seldom more; every three or four pieces of land had a house belonging to it. . . . I began to perceive the reason and nature of the thing, and found that this division of the land into small pieces, and scattering of the dwellings, was occasioned by, and done for the convenience of the business which the people were generally employed in . . . this business is the clothing trade, for the convenience of which the houses are thus scattered and spread upon the sides of the hills. . . .

He is describing here the pre-industrial landscape, or rather the pre-factory landscape of the textile industry, where the land 'in this otherwise frightful country' produced wool in abundance, and not only that but running water and coal seams even well up towards the tops of the moors, so that everything including the busy traffic flowed downhill. Every house was served by a rill of running water, and every considerable house was consequently 'a manufactory or work-house'. Hardly a house, though separated from its neighbours, stood out of speaking distance of another. And one can still see this landscape coming from the Lancashire side over the bleak sides of Heptonstall Moor.

This was a dual economy, a rational form of living that was commonly found in mining districts, whether tin in Cornwall or lead in Derbyshire, whereby a family combined farming for part of the year with mining in the rest. Here in the uplands of west Yorkshire it was a dual economy of farmer/weaver, which not only made the fullest use of the year in a difficult climate but also the fullest use of the family so that children of four or five could do their little bit towards the family economy. Truly this was a Domestic Economy. And being necessarily small farmers, with few stock (but an essential horse for carriage) their fields were also small as Defoe noticed. Such is the universal field-pattern of a countryside involved in this kind of economy.

The economy of the domestic system in cloth-weaving is revealed also in the plan and appearance of the ordinary houses, the vernacular building of the district. All these sturdy houses of Millstone Grit have a long range of windows, sometimes up to ten 'lights', on the upper floor in order to get the maximum light on the looms, especially in a climate that often produced lowering dark-grey skies (plate 79). Often, too, there is the old stable where the essential packhorse was kept, now usually a garage.

At a larger house called Greenwood Lee, west of Heptonstall, there was a further development. By its size and style it was the home of a master-clothier for whom the others, in their scattered cottages all within sight, ultimately worked. The hall, the principal living-room of the house, had added to it at the rear an extension used as a kitchen. The original kitchen had been on the same axis as the rest of the house, so why make this extension at the back? The reason was that as the cloth trade expanded, above all in the late seventeenth century, many clothiers altered their houses so that the original kitchen became the 'work-shop'. And this was done because the old through-passage from the front door to the back separated the noise and smell of the weaving from the living-rooms and also kept the latter more private from the journeymen workers. At Greenwood Lee (now a private house) the far end of the original kitchen has a mysterious feature: a narrow 'room' extending from several feet below ground up to the roof. Surely this must have been the site of a water-wheel, a still later addition. Close to the house, too, is an enormous building, as big as the house, which must have acted as a warehouse for the spun wool and the finished cloth. Other examples of such loomhouses are recorded in *The History of Working Class Housing* (ed. S. D. Chapman, 1971). The whole of this piece of country is dotted with these seventeenth- and eighteenth-century houses, mostly small farmhouses now, with their long upper mullioned windows; with here and there the grander house of the master-clothier.

Heptonstall itself is a large hill-top village, high above the Hebden Water. It is one of the most rewarding villages in the north of England, dark and dramatic, full of true native building, with its streets of stone-setts (now alas being replaced by the universal macadam) and rows of weavers' cottages. Every alley and turning in Heptonstall has its surprises. Here the hand-loom weavers had congregated in streets of small cottages, for by no means every weaver had the means to become a small farmer as well. The next step came with the invention of the power-loom driven by water, so down in the valley the domestic workshop was replaced by the full-blown factory and the town of Hebden Bridge grew up (plate 80).

Mining, too, has its characteristic landscape. In the early days it was open-cast working rather than mining, followed by shallow pits – often called 'bell-pits' from their distinctive shape – found in both the old lead and the coal areas. Plate 75 shows the extraordinary picture presented by medieval coal bell-pits from the air.

The high country of which Malham Tarn is the centre – a countryside once owned by Fountains Abbey – is most rewarding for tracking down early mining landscapes: there are early coal-pits at the northern end of Fountains Fell, copper mines near Pikedaw, iron mines, lead mines (with a remarkable smelt mill chimney on Malham Moor) and calamine mines in various places (see the map in Raistrick's *Old Yorkshire Dales*, page 127). Calamine was a grey or white powder found on the floor of caverns and of indispensable use for brassmakers. So this landscape, already described as sheep and cattle ranches developed by Fountains Abbey (chapter 2), has another aspect altogether, of a later date.

The lead workings of western Shropshire, centred upon Snailbeach (plate VI) and Gravels are perhaps the most impressive of all the visible remains of early mining. The Romans worked lead here more than eighteen hundred years ago. Pigs of lead stamped with the name of Hadrian (AD 117–38) have been found at Linley, and other workings have produced wooden shovels, candles, coins, and pottery. The Roman workings are buried under the later spoil-heaps. It is an extraordinary landscape to come across in a county usually thought of as belonging to great country houses, parkland, and rich farmland. The piles of white or greyish waste at Snailbeach can be seen from twenty miles away looking like snow-clad hills. These lead mines were worked until within living memory. At Snailbeach there are the abandoned mine-buildings, the tall chimney stacks, the torn-up railway tracks and the lonely engine-shed. The mining has gone but the visual evidence remains.

The search for lead went on higher and higher up the side of the Stiperstones. At Blackmoregate, fifteen hundred feet up on the edge of the commons, is a completely deserted settlement of small houses with their little crofts behind them. This again was a dual economy – small-scale farming which could never have paid its way alone, combined with lead mining. Only in this way could people get a living; and when the lead failed the hamlet was slowly deserted. Just like a medieval village in some ways, though the cottages here are clearly eighteenth century in date, the houses were deserted one by one. It was not until early in this century, perhaps within living memory, that the place was finally abandoned completely; and now it looks as though it had been deserted for centuries amid its sheltering sycamores and ancient hollies. It is worth the steep climb up from Snailbeach to wander round this highly atmospheric 'lost village'.

Early coal-digging is best seen on one or two Shropshire commons, as on

Catherton Common (plate 75) with its remarkable extent of old caved-in bell-pits. In Shropshire, too, is Coalbrookdale, which was described in a *History of Salop* in 1837 as 'the most extraordinary district in the world'. However we dilute this opinion, as Trevor Rowley says, it has a charisma deriving both from its beauty and its unique industrial history. Here the Severn cuts through a series of carboniferous rocks, exposing seams of coal, ironstone, clay, and limestone. Even in its early days Coalbrookdale was visited by multitudes of people 'of most ranks and stations in life'. Today it is visited by multitudes of school-parties, for it has been cleaned up and laid out, perhaps self-consciously in places; but all the same it is a monument of an early industrial landscape. The Iron Bridge, opened in 1781, has been described as probably the most outstanding industrial monument in the country; but the whole district is worth inspecting on foot, not only for the grand things but for the trivial details of the beginnings of the real Industrial Revolution.

Down in the West Country, with a totally different history and setting, is the old tin, copper, and arsenic district centred upon the gigantic wasteland called Blanchdown, west of Tavistock and high above the wooded valley of the Tamar. Here for a few decades in the nineteenth century the Devon Great Consols Mine was one of the richest copper mines in the world. In the mid-fifties Devon and Cornwall were producing more than half the world's supply of copper, and later on, when the copper was exhausted, Blanchdown produced half the world's arsenic, enough to poison the world's population – a familiar enough remark nowadays, but Victorian visitors thrilled to it.

Far below, on the banks of the Tamar where the tides just reach, a flourishing river-port grew – Morwellham. A canal carried the tin and copper ores to the top of a steep incline, and then an inclined plane brought the wagons down to the quay. All mining ceased in and round Blanchdown in the opening years of this century: today one sees a vast, broken landscape some two miles long, rich in colour from the various ores, once rich in the old machinery too. It has a fantastic beauty, worthy of John Piper's eye. But instead of the multitudes of shouting men, and the rumble of loaded wagons, it is today the silent haunt of buzzards, foxes, and harmless snakes. Morwellham, down below, was equally deserted up to a few years ago, but is now being transformed – not too brashly – into a museum of another industrial age.

Over much of neighbouring Dartmoor there are the marks of tin and copper mining, beginning with the rough scars of medieval open-cast digging, and ending with ruined engine-houses of the late Victorian days. Much of Dartmoor, like so many of the high Yorkshire moors, is really a disguised industrial landscape. So, more obviously, is the greater part of Cornwall, with its long history of tin and copper working, beginning with tin in prehistoric times. Many books have been written about Cornish mining, the decay of which has produced huge, deeply melancholy landscapes, for besides the spectacle of ruined mine-buildings, often standing on the skyline and deeply moving when dusk falls, there is also the extraordinary atmosphere that even the most insensitive must feel of a Lost Country. There is a magic in western Cornwall which the remains of a once-busy industrial landscape only deepens.

75 Medieval coal-mining was on a small scale. Often it was open working, like the Cornish and Devon tin-works, but in places small shafts were sunk and men worked around at the bottom eventually producing an underground bell-shape. These 'bell-pits', of no great depth, caved in at the top when they fell into disuse, so producing this very odd appearance from the air. This scene is at Lubberland on Catherton Common in Shropshire. Commons were often exploited for this purpose as the minerals belonged to the lord of the manor.

76   Tin has been worked in Cornwall since prehistoric times. In the first half of the nineteenth century it was a flourishing industry. Now only two mines are worked, and the landscape, especially in the west, is studded with these ruined engine-houses and stacks. It is a melancholy scene, especially at evening when the ruins stand out windowless and broken. Some of the Cornish engine-houses are such fine industrial buildings that they have been scheduled as ancient monuments.

77   After the tin, came the great copper boom, especially in west Cornwall. Dolcoath, shown here, was going strong in the 1720s but in the 1830s, the date of this drawing, it was on the decline. Oddly enough, though, tin was found beneath the worked-out copper and gave the mine a second life. When it finally closed in 1920 it had become the deepest mine in Cornwall (over 550 fathoms) and had produced some 350,000 tons of copper ore and over 80,000 tons of black tin.

78   An old lead-mining landscape at Greenhow in Yorkshire. The Romans worked lead up here towards the end of the first century. Mining went on for many centuries but is now ended. The landscape is one of miners' cottages and small intakes, since in England most small-scale mining (lead, tin, coal and so forth) was carried on with small-scale farming: a dual economy. There are shaft-heaps and ruined smelt-mills and dressing plants on the moors or down in the valleys.

79   In the West Riding especially the textile industry was very much a rural occupation, as Defoe noted in his travels round England. Then the weavers congregated in the villages like Golcar, shown here, and their cottages can be recognised at once by the long upper windows, so made to throw the maximum light on the loom. This is a seven-light window, divided by stout mullions of the local Millstone Grit. Some of the best examples of this type of 'industrial building' can be seen in and round Heptonstall, to the west of Halifax. All used the hand-loom, in their own houses, with no other power.

80 With the coming of water-power in the late eighteenth century the textile industry shifted down from the hills, as at Heptonstall, into the deep valleys like this one at Hebden Bridge. Here a fast-flowing river attracted newer and larger mills and one of the early industrial towns was born, with its acres of closely-packed working-class housing climbing up the hillsides, reserving the waterside for the mills. The Rochdale Canal (see colour plate VIII) opened to Hebden Bridge in 1798 also stimulated the industrial landscape along its banks.

England is a small and crowded country, rich in the monuments of the past since it has been so little fought over. But every year sees the rate of destruction increase. The motorways creep inexorably over unravished landscapes. They have to fight every inch of the way through public inquiries but they invariably win. All one can say in their favour is that this trail of excavation is revealing archaeological sites hitherto unsuspected, completely unknown, at an astonishing rate. Every mile is turning up evidence of a past settlement or some other buried evidence in areas that showed nothing on the surface. The evidence has to be examined under bad and hurried conditions but in a sense it is gratuitous information about past landscapes which we might never otherwise have known. Out of evil comes forth some good; just as the hated presence of the Army on the most beautiful coast of Dorset has in its odd way saved large tracts of ancient field-systems from what would have been inevitable building development and the complete erosion of the archaeological evidence. And there are stretches of motorway that enhance the modern landscape (as well as others that utterly befoul it). One wonders what archaeological sites were smashed to pieces by the railways in their time, with their massive embankments and cuttings, not to mention their more unspectacular stretches through settled areas.

The country houses decay and fall. Some are totally demolished but often they are left behind a curtain of barbed wire to rot slowly in the English rain and wind and frost. As such they are melancholy memorials of a lost civilisation, for such it was at its best (plate 81). Thousands of miles of hedgerows are bulldozed out of existence every year in the interests of a highly-mechanised farming; but even from this the landscape-historian can derive a certain pleasure for he sees an open-field landscape coming back after having disappeared for some two hundred years: not in the same detail of course, but the general effect (regardless of the economic arguments against this kind of erosion) is that of long sweeping lines running for miles as they used to do. In town and country 'listed' buildings – those of historic and/or architectural interest – go by the hundred every year despite a theoretical protection.

And finally there is the systematic destruction of the railways (plate 74) which produces a new feature in the landscape, above all in the old cuttings through hilly country. Here a variety of shrubs, weeds, and wild flowers flourish in more or less sheltered conditions. Within ten years nature takes over again.

The decay of the canals began earlier. Few survived into the second half of the twentieth century, and where they do they offer miles of deserted towpaths and safe walking, the haunt of water-birds, the quiet angler, and the family picnic. They form a sort of human conservancy, better perhaps than any one designated officially, for it has come about naturally and by accident.

Despite the catalogue of destruction and decay in our times, and one could go on with a long tale of horror and woe, so much is left to study and enjoy.

Indeed, after fifty years of exploring English landscapes I am left with one abiding impression and that is the tremendous continuity of life in this country, a continuity that is sometimes clearly visible as at Portchester in Hampshire (plate 82), one of the most remarkable monuments in this country. Here the Normans built a great castle and a small church inside the almost-complete walls of a Roman fort of the late fourth century. And what of the earthworks outside the walls of the castle, and what lies underneath the large open space in the middle of the Roman fort? Has Portchester an even longer history than we can see above ground?

Often the continuity of a piece of landscape or a settlement is hidden, as in the Fenland, so apparently devoid of any historic interest at first sight. To many, it is simply a dull tract of country that stretches away to a far horizon, swept by bitter winds (see front cover) yet the work of the past two or three decades has shown it to be one of the most fascinating buried landscapes in Europe. Or take Long Melford, that beautiful street-village in Suffolk, which has, one would think, quite enough to delight the explorer above ground. In 1958, when drains were being laid at the backs of houses along the whole length of the south-western side of this street, it was revealed that a Belgic and Roman settlement occupied virtually the whole of this stretch. What else lies buried under the occupied houses and other dwellings we shall only know by chance in the future; but it seems certain from this accidental discovery that Long Melford existed as far back as Belgic times and that it has been inhabited continuously ever since. There must be hundreds, if not thousands, of English villages – despite their Old English or Scandinavian names – that stand on sites first chosen in Roman and pre-Roman times.

A few miles up the broad estuary of the Exe in south Devon stands the little town of Topsham (plate 83) sheltered by a low ridge behind it, with warm, light, and fertile soils, a place with an impeccable English name. But it was also the port for Roman Exeter, *Isca Dumnoniorum*. Its own Roman name has been forgotten long ago. Yet even this is not all, for a copper double-axe has been found just outside the town of the same type as those found on the Acropolis in Athens and at Mycenae, dating from about 1250 BC. The Topsham axe was undoubtedly made in the Aegean, and traders from the Eastern Mediterranean were sailing up this estuary more than three thousand years ago to the strand of some prehistoric settlement:

> Shy traffickers, the dark Iberians come;
> And on the beach undid their corded bales.

Beneath the Saxon layer, the Roman, and beneath that again the links with Bronze Age Greece. There is no reason to suppose that this delectable spot has ever been deserted by man since the days when the Aegean ships found their way up this shining, sunlit estuary so long ago.

There is then this long continuity in the English landscape, in many favoured parts at least. We now know that in the fertile Vale of Evesham there is plenty of evidence for widespread peasant farming round Pershore and Evesham from Romano-British times onwards. And one of the most remarkable discoveries of the past twenty years or so has been the revelation that the gravels along the edge of the Fenland between Peterborough and Bourne in Lincolnshire — and especially beside the river Welland — have been intensively and continuously occupied during the past five thousand years. Because of the widespread commercial gravel diggings much has already been uncovered; and much more shows up from the air — the outlines of former roadways, fields, farmsteads, and burial mounds all show clearly as dark marks in the growing crops in a dry summer (*Early Man in the Welland Valley*, 1966 report).

Nor is it only buried evidence that leads one to see deeper layers beneath the apparently obvious. Near Bourne is the fen-edge village of Thurlby, a pure Scandinavian place-name with the meaning of 'Thurulf's village', apparently a settlement that followed the Danish Conquest of 876 and the partition of Mercia. But just outside the village to the east runs the Roman canal called the Car Dyke, here a broken-down and rather murky stretch, and on the very bank of this canal stands the parish church with the unique dedication of St Firmin. Firmin was a third-century bishop in Gaul. Some Roman landlord from Gaul, or who knew Gaul, must surely have imported this saintly name to this faraway Lincolnshire village, long before the invading Danes took over and Thurulf gave his own name to an already settled place. Everything is older than we think.

The more or less systematic planning of the landscape over large tracts of open-field England, mostly between about 1700 and 1820, has already been discussed; but even this large-scale attempt to remodel the landscape generally left on one side the commons and wastes as being basically uprofitable except for rough grazing, and not always even that. Even so, more than five hundred acts of Parliament between 1760 and 1800 tamed commons and wastes to the extent of three-quarters of a million acres; and with the need for more food during the Napoleonic Wars the pace of enclosure of the commons intensified. When the wars were over the teeming millions of the industrial towns also had to be fed: they were consumers of food and not producers, unlike their ancestors a generation or so earlier. In all, we lost well over two million acres of open spaces — high moorlands and lowland heaths — yet the effect on the landscape was not as dramatic as these figures would suggest. On some of the high moors of the North drystone walls appeared, right up to the summits (plate 60), and the moorland was technically enclosed. But apart from the walls, which now seem an immemorial part of the scene, nothing much else changed. Bodmin Moor in Cornwall (plate 84) remains much as it always has been since prehistoric times, except that in many places the poor grassland has been improved and some patches of marsh dangerous to cattle and sheep have been drained.

Not all the commons and wastes were in the uplands. The poor sandy and gravelly soils of some of the Home Counties, even on the very edge of London, were very largely common land with its own characteristic vegetation. These, too, have been left more or less untouched, though at times only as the result of memorable battles against landlords anxious to 'develop' the land for housing the growing millions of London. Wimbledon Common and Hampstead Heath produced memorable battles; so too did Epping Forest. Ancient landscapes thus survive within the bounds of London itself. Over England as a whole more than a million acres of land are still open commons, but they are coming under pressure. One of the lowland commons of eastern Dorset – Winfrith Heath – nearly six hundred acres in extent, is now the site of an Atomic Energy Station; but even the government had to pass a special act of Parliament to extinguish the ancient common rights officially before it could build upon the Heath.

It was of one of these Dorset lowland heaths that Thomas Hardy wrote in *The Return of the Native*:

> In fact, precisely at this transitional point of its nightly roll into darkness the great and particular glory of the Egdon waste began, and nobody could be said to understand the heath who had not been there at such a time. . . . The great inviolate place had an ancient permanence which the sea cannot claim. . . . The sea changed, the rivers, the villages, and the people changed, yet Egdon remained.

Among the distinctive landscapes of England these brooding Dorset heath-lands are among the oldest and the least touched by man. In some parts of England, like the Fenland, we still have an ancient landscape – 'one of the most completely recognisable ancient landscapes in Western Europe' as has been said earlier – but it is for the most part buried today and only the aerial photographer or the archaeologist can really see beneath its surface. The Fenlands have been much altered by man over thousands of years: but on Egdon and the neighbouring heaths man has achieved little or nothing. It is all as it was in the beginning.

81 Butleigh Court in Somerset was one of the many country houses built during the reign of Victoria by a prosperous squirearchy. Built in 1850, it was abandoned in less than ninety years when the last squire died. In 1947 the lead was stolen from the roof, and nature took over the ruins. Within twenty-five years the abandoned house is festooned with creepers inside and out, and it looks as though it has been empty ever since the Black Death.

82　　Portchester is the sort of place one would go hundreds of miles to see if it were in some foreign country; and it is also a splendid example of the long continuity of English life. What we see here is the best of the Roman forts of the Saxon Shore, built about 300 AD and almost perfectly preserved. Inside it the Normans put up a splendid castle, mostly dating from the time of Henry II (1154–89) and a perfect little church in the 1130s. The Normans took over the outer walls of the Roman Fort as their outer bailey. Whether the Fort was ever wholly abandoned in Saxon times we do not yet know: probably not. And outside the Roman walls, in the little town of Portchester, life carries on.

83   Topsham, where the Exe broadens out to the sea, is another example of the continuity of life in this country. Its present name – 'Toppa's *ham*' – is Saxon and quite uninformative, but we know it was the Roman port of Exeter with a now-forgotten name. And on the end of the peninsula (top right) a Bronze Age axe has been found. With fertile soils, on a wide estuary facing south, and a genial climate, there is no reason why this site should ever have been abandoned over the last four thousand years.

84   Untouched moorland below Rough Tor on Bodmin Moor in Cornwall. This is still common land, pasturage for cattle as it has been since neolithic times, with no fences in sight (they are illegal on common land) and no human habitation. There are at least a million acres of common land left in England alone, though a good deal of it lies now in urban areas. But this remains as it always was, except for the improved horses. Once wild horses roamed here; their descendants survive on Dartmoor but not here.